THE MYSTERY OF THE WORD

By the Author of
The Mystery of Marriage

The Mystery of the *Word*

Parables of Everyday Faith

Mike Mason

1817

Harper & Row, Publishers, San Francisco

Cambridge, Hagerstown, New York, Philadelphia, Washington
London, Mexico City, São Paulo, Singapore, Sydney

The story "The Changeling" appeared in somewhat different form in *Crux* 19, no. 4 (December 1983): 11–15.

Scripture quotations are from the Holy Bible, New International Bible Society. Copyright © 1973, 1978, 1984 International Bible Society. Used by permission of Zondervan Bible Publishers. Occasionally Scripture references are paraphrased by the author.

FIRST EDITION

Library of Congress Cataloging-in-Publication Data

Mason, Mike, 1953–
    The mystery of the word.

    1. Christian fiction. 2. Parables. 3. Meditations. 4. Storytelling—Religious aspects—Christianity. I. Title.
PR9199.3.M3927M97 1988   242   87-46218
ISBN 0-06-065469-4

---

88 89 90 91 92 RRD 10 9 8 7 6 5 4 3 2 1

For my father and mother,
lovers of stories

Contents

Jesus spoke all these things to the crowd in parables;
He did not say anything to them without using a parable.

—MATTHEW 13:34

This book is writ in such a dialect
As may the minds of listless men affect:
It seems a novelty, and yet contains
Nothing but sound and honest gospel strains.

—JOHN BUNYAN
Author's Apology to
The Pilgrim's Progress

Introduction:
A Word on Christian
Fiction

To what shall we compare the Kingdom of God? Or what parable shall we use to describe it?

—MARK 4:30

In these words of Jesus is there perhaps a note of frustration present—or at the very least a certain wistfulness? Is it not almost a rhetorical question He is posing? For strictly speaking the Kingdom of God is something that bears no comparison and for which no amount of word magic is adequate.

As it turns out, however, the Master's question is not such a rhetorical one after all, since throughout the gospels He answers it again and again, in comparison after comparison, metaphor after metaphor, parable after parable. It is simply a part of the wonder of the Incarnation that that which surpasses understanding should be rendered understandable and that divine secrets should stoop to take on flesh—the flesh of human language. Yet how surprising it is to discover that the Almighty God is not nebulous and silent, but is a speaker! And even more surprisingly, He is a writer.

Such is the mystery of the Word: that in spite of all the fragility, the corruptibility, the maddening subjectivity and imprecision of the medium of language, nevertheless the Lord of the universe has entrusted Himself to it. Not only has He delivered speeches but He has caused those speeches to be recorded, thus committing Himself to paper. His good news has been published! Moreover, when we examine this writing of God, we find that it takes the form not of some obscure religious treatise but rather of a collection of stories, images, riddles, songs, poems, journalism and history, with even a few family trees and shopping lists thrown in. Pure theology, as it happens, figures much less prominently in Holy Scripture than might be expected, suggesting that God the Author is not so much a theologian as He is a writer of *literature* in the broadest sense of that word. And similarly, when the Son of God came into the world, He came as a storyteller as much as a preacher.

In fact, in Matthew 13:34 we are told that "Jesus spoke all these things to the crowd in parables; He did not say anything to them without using a parable." This is a startling verse. Paraphrased, it might read: "Jesus didn't preach to the people. Instead He just told them stories all day long."

How many preachers do we know like that today? To be sure, most preachers like to spice up their sermons with a few of what are termed in the jargon (perhaps somewhat deprecatingly) "illustrations"—a personal recollection here and there, a colorful anecdote, a missionary story, or a good joke.

But how many preachers would risk climbing into their pulpit of a Sunday morning and delivering their entire message in the form of stories? *Risk* is an appropriate word here, for to many pastors such an experiment might seem tantamount to preaching with both hands tied behind the back. It would mean putting all the homiletical eggs in one basket. And who today trusts the gospel that much? Who has ever heard of a gospel that might actually be inherently persuasive enough to *preach itself?*

No, we are an explanation-oriented people. We want information, answers, bald statements, rational theology. We are a little like the New Testament Pharisees who, driven to distraction by Jesus' incessant fiddling around with allusive, figurative language, demanded of Him, "How long will you keep us in suspense? If you are the Christ, tell us plainly!" To which Jesus responded, as plainly as anyone could wish, "'I did tell you, but you do not believe'" (John 10:24–25).

Of course Jesus in His teaching did more than tell stories and weave metaphors. He also preached the gospel discursively and analytically. But any balanced view of His evangelistic methods must come to terms with the fact that close to one third of His entire oral ministry consisted of pure storytelling. Parables and parabolic language are sprinkled like jewels throughout the gospels, but they also occur in heavy concentrations—for example, in Matthew 13 (commonly known as the sermon of parables) or in Luke 14–16, where no less than three long chapters in a row are given over to nearly continuous storytelling.

What this means, in effect, is that a great deal of what Jesus said is *not literally true*. The parables are *fiction*, works of the imagination that Jesus made up (or, if you like, heard on His Father's knee), and the truth they contain is an imaginative or spiritual truth. Apparently there were frequent occasions in the Lord's ministry when He sensed that this parabolic strategy was called for, when for one reason or another He felt reluctant to "tell it like it is" and chose rather to speak more indirectly. Were these times, perhaps, of particular resistance to His message, times when the people were so restless, so complacent, or so hardened and hostile that the only thing that held any hope of getting the hook in their hearts was a story?

Or was it, one wonders, primarily the unanswerable, nonplussing quality of storytelling that Jesus valued? The best theology, after all, and the most clearly presented doctrine always leave room for (and even invite) argument. But a parable shuts mouths. To a good story there is no answer. At least, if the point of a powerful piece of fiction is to be disputed, it must be disputed in its own terms—with creativity, freshness, subtlety, depth, and charm. A Pharisee is simply not capable of such qualities.

In any case, whatever Jesus' strategy may have been, it is a matter of record that He at times spoke to the crowd in fiction, and He did not say anything to them except in the form of fiction, and often enough the only explanation He deigned to offer was, "He who has ears, let him hear" (Matt. 13:9). And there were many other means too, besides storytelling, by which Jesus accepted the profound discipline and humility of letting the gospel speak for itself.

Right here lies the mandate for Christian fiction, the scriptural injunction for Christians to be following the example of Jesus (and of the Bible as a whole) by actively engaging not only in the writing and telling of stories but also in other artful works of the imagination. For it is not just that fiction (or art in general) can occasionally be a useful channel for presenting the gospel or can provide colorful "illustrations." Far more than that, there are times and places when *fiction alone* can effectively communicate the truth. There are times when the genius of communication lies not in direct statement but rather in indirection and concealment.

In view of all the scriptural support behind pure storytelling as an indispensable tool for the Church, why is it that Christians (and particularly orthodox believers) have so often adopted a suspicious, reactionary, and even iconoclastic stand when it comes to the production of good fiction? As a Christian practitioner of this demanding art, I must admit that I feel somewhat like a certain Canadian Jesuit, Father Bauer, who is quite well known for having been the coach of that country's first Olympic hockey team. For I can't help wondering about this man: what is a Jesuit priest doing coaching hockey? And yet it's the same sort of dilemma for the Christian writer of fiction; it's like trying to skate and stickhandle while wearing a long black robe.

This book began, therefore, simply as a collection of short stories. I wanted to let the gospel speak for itself. However, since the writing of serious, realistic fiction (in contrast to the genres of poetry, fantasy, science fiction, or allegory) has been such a neglected and misunderstood craft among Christians, I eventually decided to append to each of my fictional pieces a few pages of nonfictional material, short meditations focusing on the theme of storytelling and its place in biblical faith. These meditations, while they comment directly on the content of the accompanying stories, do so more for purposes of reflection than of interpretation.

The resulting book is admittedly a hybrid and something of a compromise. It is a hodgepodge of fiction and nonfiction, two distinct genres that, in the minds of both literary and theological purists, mix like oil and water. However, for the Christian writer who takes the Word of God as a handbook of literature as well as of life, it turns out that the rigid boundaries between the various literary forms may not be quite so clear-cut as the world has made them. For the Bible itself is a hodgepodge of forms. No pleasingly integrated artistic whole, it is instead an unlikely grab bag of miscellanies, in which each separate "book" (most of which are not books at all, but pamphlets) does not so much conform to an already existing genre as explode into a brand new genre of its own. For new wine is not put into old skins. The epistles may be thought of as being cast in the form of letters, but who else ever sent or received letters such as these? And what, after all, is a *gospel*?

As for the term *parable*, it turns out that the Bible's definition of this unique genre is a very loose one indeed. For in actual biblical usage the term may be applied to anything from a single image ("I am the light of the world") to an entire book (such as Jonah). Even within the gospels alone parables range all the way from simple similes ("The Kingdom of Heaven is like yeast") to expanded metaphors ("I am the vine, you are the branches . . .") to neatly integrated sermon illustrations (such as the parable of the two sons in Matthew 21), to full-fledged allegories (the parable of the weeds in Matthew 13), to more elaborate stories that cannot, indeed must not, be interpreted allegorically (the parable of the dishonest steward in Luke 16).

Again, if we try to classify this peculiar genre according to its manner of conveying religious teaching, we find that parables can sometimes be blatant moral tales in which the fictional art is but a thinly veiled "excuse" for sermonizing (see the parable of the sheep and the goats in Matthew 25); or at the other extreme parables may be highly sophisticated narratives so finely and artistically woven that whatever "moral" they contain simply cannot be separated out from the story itself—as in the case of the parable of the prodigal son, in which the medium *is* the message.

Biblical parable, furthermore, may take a dramatic as well as a narrative form. Throughout Jesus' ministry we see Him not only *telling* parables but *enacting* them, whether it be in the cursing of a fig tree, in the washing of His disciples' feet, or in the laying down of His life for the salvation of the world. Indeed, when Matthew tries to explain to us the significance of Jesus' parabolic ministry, he says that it was in fulfillment of the prophecy in Psalm 78:2: "I will open my mouth in parables" (Matt. 13:35). Yet when we examine this lengthy psalm in its Old Testament context we find that it does not contain any fictional "story-parables" at all. Instead what the Psalmist meant was that he was going to give a history lesson, a literal account of God's dealings with Israel from the Exodus up to the time of David. Here "history" becomes "His-story," God's great novel written not in mere words but in the fleshed-out experience of His people. These were parables that really happened!

Clearly the rather narrow, conventional literary definition of what a parable ought to be like is simply far too rigid to have much relevance within the wild context of Scripture, and from this fact I have taken courage to call my own book a collection of "parables." Moreover, as Jesus Himself was not averse to adding a few words of commentary to His stories, I have done the same. If the resulting patchwork suffers artistically for being an ungainly mixture of fiction and nonfiction, seeming to scrabble along like some sort of black-skirted priest on ice skates, then let it be so. God's grace is sufficient.

Mamba

I t was a night to make a man realize how totally depen-
dent the world is on light from above. We were up in the
Yukon, forty miles from anywhere, and the sky was as
black as the earth.

There were just the two of us, backpacking. We'd come a
long way that day, filled with a peculiar energy, and had kept
on hiking far into the long northern twilight. Then suddenly a
bank of clouds had rolled in and the night had descended like
a black hood. Even the trees right beside the trail disappeared,
as if with the failing of the light they ceased to exist. For all
we could see in front of us we might have been standing on
the lip of a precipice. You could feel the darkness like soot
lining your nostrils, coating the inside of your mouth. There
was something almost unnatural about it.

We stopped and got a fire going. The first flames sank into
the night like water into sand, but soon, as the sticks began to
crackle, a room appeared in the forest, a little cave of light.
While Alex got some food together I pitched the tent, stealing
glances at this man I had been with on the trail for the past
four days. I was still shy, still somewhat in awe of him. He
whistled, and his white hair gleamed, and in the firelight his
tall enormous body looked even larger, welded to his shadow
as it flashed among the trees like a supernatural being. If I
were a grizzly bear, wouldn't I stay away from this man?

Alex was a white African who for thirty years had been a
missionary in Angola and Zambia. There was a certain charis-
ma about him, but beyond that he struck me as having a quality for which the only name I could think of was *Christ-
likeness*. It came out of his pores, almost, as if it were a physi-

cal characteristic, and it made me uneasy about the fact that I had never been able to make my peace with the Christian faith. It wasn't that he'd pressed me, nor even that we'd done a lot of talking about religion. On the contrary, every night around the campfire Alex had regaled me with stories about hunting. Born in Rhodesia, he had hunted as a boy in the Zambezi Valley. Later he'd lived with a tribe of Kaonde, and he told me the sort of tales that, if only they could have been written down just the way he told them, would have curled Hemingway's hair.

I kept thinking, here is this man who more than anyone I've ever met reminds me of Jesus Christ—and he's telling me stories about big game hunting! But then, there we were way up in the Yukon Territory, probably the best place in all of North America to sit around a campfire of an evening and hear some real stories.

"If we were camping out in the bush in Africa," Alex had said one night, "we could shine our torches all around into the trees and pick out the eyes of the lions and hyenas, like green and orange jewels. You don't dare let your fire go out, especially when there's fresh-killed game in the camp. And if you're out hunting with the Kaonde and you go to bed before midnight, you miss everything. That's when Africans really come alive, when they drop their guard and begin to reveal themselves. And you should hear the stories then!"

Was it the stories as much as the fires, I wondered, that kept the lions at bay?

"Of course, things are not so very different in North America," Alex continued. "Here too, if you really want to loosen a man's tongue and get to know him, you have to sit up together after midnight."

Preferably with a bottle of scotch, I thought, although I didn't say this to Alex. But maybe the scotch was just window dressing, and it was really the night that coaxed people out of their shells . . . .

"I suppose over here it's also true," I heard myself say, "that if you shine a light out into the darkness, out past the civilized, firelit circle of your own close-knit camp, you can almost see the eyes of the wild beasts glaring at you." It was one of those thoughts that just came to one, out of nowhere, while gazing into a campfire.

So far on this hike we had done a good job of getting to bed early. But this night, the night of the unusual darkness, following supper we were still wide awake. The strange energy of the day continued to pulse and quiver inside us. We had a second and then a third cup of coffee. And when Alex's talk turned to snakes, my ears grew as big as our two shadows dancing against the forest wall.

He told a story about traveling to a remote village in central Zambia to teach a Bible class. He and about a dozen Zambians had been gathered in a small hut with a thatched roof. The lesson—of all things—happened to be on the last chapter of the Book of Acts, in which Paul, shipwrecked on Malta, is bitten by a poisonous snake. But no sooner had Alex opened his Bible and begun to speak than the Africans jumped to their feet and ran out of the hut, leaving him all alone.

"It was the strangest thing," he related. "I couldn't figure it out. You'd have thought the place had burst into flames. I went outside and there they all were, standing about a hundred yards from the hut and shuffling their bare feet, staring at me. 'What's wrong?' I called out. 'Is my teaching that bad?' But no one would say a thing. I walked straight up to them and asked again, 'What's the matter with you?' Finally the oldest man raised his arm, and pointing to the hut said one word: '*Mamba.*' There was dead silence, like the silence just after someone has screamed in the night, as we all froze before the meaning of this word. I was the only man with my back to the hut."

"Mamba," I said slowly, as Alex paused to sip his coffee. "Mamba." I let the sound of the word form a physical impression on my lips and tongue. "Isn't that the deadliest snake in the world?"

"Very close," replied Alex. "It's certainly the most feared snake in Africa. The king cobra comes larger, but the black mamba is faster. It's said that the mamba can travel at the speed of a galloping horse, although I think that's an exaggeration. Still, to see one of these creatures in full flight across an open plain is something. It's like greased lightning. And one snake carries enough venom to kill a dozen men. It's an extremely potent neurotoxin, causing paralysis and death within six to twenty minutes. I once heard a story about a mamba being cornered by five cows. Suddenly the snake lashed out and struck all five, just like electricity, and inside of twenty minutes every one of those cows lay dead. Five cows—imagine! So that's the sort of creature this is. And as I stood in front of those Bible students that day, I knew that every one of them had one or more relatives who had been killed by the mamba. They had never heard of anyone surviving a bite."

"So what did you do?" I asked.

"What *could* I do? A kind of fear had come over me, and yet I knew it was not primarily a fear of the snake but rather a fear of the Lord. It is a quiet, uncanny sort of feeling, something I have come to recognize as the Spirit of God moving in me. So right away I knew what I had to do. My whole purpose in being there, after all, was to be a witness to the God of creation, and that very day we were to study a passage in His Word about the Apostle Paul being bitten by a deadly viper yet suffering no ill effects. Now I wasn't about to let myself be bitten by this mamba, but at the same time I didn't feel I could just run away. Either God had power over the whole world of nature, including poisonous snakes, or He didn't.

"So very gingerly I returned to that hut, opened the door, and peered into the gloom. It took a while for my eyes to adjust again, and even then I saw nothing. But I wasn't looking in the right place. I had to go right inside, and just knowing the thing was there, I could nearly smell it; more like a spirit, it was, than a body. Finally I looked up—it was a thatched ceiling, open all around the edges—and there, sure enough, draped across one of the rafters, was a full-grown black mamba, over ten feet long. Though I'd lived in Africa all my life, it was the first time I'd ever seen one in the wild. He looked very relaxed, self-assured. Yet I knew he must be more frightened than I was. Man, you know, is the most poisonous creature of all.

"Well, I had often experienced in the past the way the Lord likes to accompany the preaching of His Word with an object lesson. So going back to my group of students, almost before I realized what I was doing, I opened my mouth and said, 'Who will come and help me fight the mamba?' By this time the whole village had begun to gather round, and I kept asking for a volunteer. I read to them the passage about Paul and the viper and preached on it. I was astounded at my own boldness. Of course I knew very little about mambas at that stage. I'd heard a few horror stories, but no one I'd known personally had ever been killed. So I preached my heart out, and not one person came forward to offer help. All the eyes kept avoiding mine, looking down at the dust or staring past me towards the hut. Finally the local pastor spoke up, with words I'll never forget: 'Bwana,' he said, 'you go—we'll pray.'

"Well, that's the way it is when you're a missionary. It's what everyone says to you: 'Bwana, you go—we'll pray.' Certainly I had no doubt that these fellows would pray. That was something they were good at. They were far from being a mature bunch of Christians, but they certainly believed—unlike North Americans—in spiritual power, both black and white. One of the men handed me a spear, and as I walked back alone towards that hut a prayer meeting started up behind me the likes of which you've never heard over here. Those Africans, you know, they make even your Pentecostals look like a waxworks. Yet even with all of that ruckus going on outside, the moment I stepped over the threshold of the hut it seemed quiet as a tomb. There was just me and the mamba in there, and a six-foot-long spear.

"Standing up on the table in the middle of the room, I surveyed the situation. I recall being amazed at how slender the snake was, just like a carriage whip. But I'd speared a few snakes before this, and although I was afraid I also had a buoyant, preposterous sense of overconfidence. It's a fine line, you know, between courage and foolhardiness. From the table I hauled myself up onto one of the rafters, trying to act very casual, just as if I were climbing up there to serve tea or something. But all at once it came over me: here I was eyeball to eyeball with a legend! It was like the feeling I'd had when I first encountered a rhino, a lion, or any of the truly dangerous game. It's the supreme thrill of hunting, this face-to-face showdown with the utterly untamed. It's the thrill of having fear like a taste upon your lips and yet mastering that.

"At the same time I sensed something about this mamba that seemed to put it in a class of its own, different from anything else I'd ever hunted. Snakes are eerie creatures to begin with—no legs or arms, all mouth and stomach, eyes like gleaming empty sockets—and looking at that thing up there on the rafter, I had a sensation, just for a moment, of being transfixed, too fascinated to move, as if the mamba could somehow paralyze even before it struck. It's a feeling I've noticed before in the presence of something—or someone—not just dangerous, but evil. I was close enough to that snake that I could actually hear him breathe. He wasn't hissing—not yet—but his mouth was half-open, and the little tongue was flickering back and forth like a tiny flame of fire.

"The black mamba, by the way, is really not very black at all, more a dark metallic gray, but the inside of the mouth is black as pitch, just as if it's been painted, and there are two large fangs so far forward they're almost under the snout. The mouth stretches around for about 330 degrees, I'd say, nearly slicing the head in half. And the shape of that head will be forever imprinted on my brain. It's a flat-topped, elongated hexagon, exactly like a coffin. All in all, this is a creature with the most malevolent expression I've ever seen on a face, and I have no trouble understanding why in the Bible the devil takes the form of a serpent.

"Sizing up the mamba took only seconds, of course. Whether or not he was in a mood to strike, I didn't know. Normally a mamba will strike as soon as he's threatened. But they're very uncertain of temper. I suppose we might have stared at each other all day, lounging up there on the rafters, so finally I just said a prayer, took a deep breath, and let it out slowly—much the way you aim with a rifle—and then, not letting go of the end of the spear, I thrust it straight at the mamba's head. This was a trick I'd learned with snakes: always aim for the head. In fact, aim for the tongue. Even if you're using a gun, aim for that little flicking tongue and you've got a good chance of hitting the thing dead in the mouth. Because a snake, when it sees something coming, will go for it. And a snake like the mamba can strike faster than a bullet.

"So I went for the head, and what do you know? I missed! So much for the tricks of hunting. I hate to think what would have happened if I'd missed altogether, but as it was, I nailed the thing to the rafter right in the middle of its body, and immediately it flew into a rage and began lashing out at me, first with the head and then with the tail, twisting back and forth like a live fuse lit at both ends. It was the most incredible display of fury I've ever seen, just as if the breath of hell had been unleashed against me, an actual wind of black and putrid violence. Luckily by leaning back as far as I could I was able to keep just inches out of reach. But the hissing alone was enough to send shivers up a dead man's spine. It completely unmanned me. Terror gripped the pit of my stomach like a fist, and my muscles turned to water. It was all I could do just to hold onto that spear, though I dared not let go. According to the story in Acts, the Apostle Paul had simply brushed his viper off like a little mosquito. But somehow this

situation was different. For doesn't Scripture also say, 'Do not
put the Lord thy God to the test'? What a brazen fool I'd
been! I was just a young man, twenty-four at the time, and
suddenly I'd taken on more than I could handle. I had thrown
away my whole life!

"'O Lord!' I cried out. 'What am I going to do now?' And
then I simply began to holler for help at the top of my lungs.
The snake hissed and squirmed, and I too squealed like a
stuck pig, and the two of us carried on like that for several
minutes. I might as well have been nailed to the rafter myself.
And as for those Africans—my cries must have been drowned
out by the loudness of their praying. But finally the oldest
man of the tribe approached the hut and poked his head in
the window, a little white-haired black face withered up like a
raisin.

"'Get me a machete!' I yelled at him. 'I have to have a
machete!' When the fellow returned it was not with a machete
but with a short wooden club, which he handed up to me gingerly, and then he disappeared again like a flash. And for the
next hour I flailed the air with that useless club. Every time
the snake's head came within reach I swung at it. But how do
you hit something that can move faster than a bullet? My arm
began to feel as if it would fall off. At that point I tried holding the butt of the spear against my body and swinging the
club with both hands. But that nearly killed me. Finally I was
at my wits' end. What more could I do? I was too exhausted
to continue. So, muttering a final prayer in desperation, I released my pressure on the spear and let the snake drop. By
that time I think I honestly believed he had wings and would
fly up straight into my face! But to my great surprise, the
thing curled up on the floor and didn't make another move. I
suppose he was exhausted too. And so there we were again,
quietly staring at one another.

"Immediately I began to plot how I could inch along the rafter and slip out the top of the window. But at the same time
another plan was forming in my mind. For as bone weary as I

was, a man hates to give up—especially with an audience! So, reaching above me and pulling out a handful of thatch from the roof, I threw it down at the snake, just to see what he would do. Well, he backed away. Then I threw more handfuls, and he kept retreating, and before long I had him backed into a corner right beside a filing cabinet that I knew was heavily loaded with Bible-study materials. All the while I had been crawling along the rafter until I was just above the cabinet, and finally I hung my feet down and pushed against it for all I was worth. The metal cabinet came down with a great crash and landed right on top of the mamba, leaving just his head sticking out. I doubt whether he was solidly pinned, but it did buy me a couple of seconds, enough time to drop to the floor with my spear and let it fly. And this time the point went straight down the snake's throat.

"It was the last ounce of strength I had. Like an empty sack I collapsed on the floor beside the dead mamba. How the Africans knew that the coast was now clear, I have no idea, but in no time the whole bunch of them came flooding into the hut, cheering and wanting to clap me on the back. The Lord had given me a great victory over the mamba, they kept saying. But in all honesty, that's not the way I felt. What sort of victory is it that leaves you feeling drained and defeated? Also I was angry that no one had come to help me, and I pleaded with everyone just to go away and leave me alone. If I'd had any desire to be a hero, I was reminded that day that God is not in the business of making heroes. All I wanted was to get home to my own bed and sleep the clock around, which is exactly what I did. There was no more Bible class that day."

Our fire had burned down to the point where all I could see of Alex was his face, suspended in the night. His skin was a rosy white, but in his features there was something negroid: broad nose, full lips, eyes the colour of mud. And it was a face so round and large that I felt the way a child might feel looking up into the face of its father. I desperately wanted to relate to this man as an equal yet knew I could not. What is there to say to someone who has fought with a dragon in order to defend the truthfulness of God?

The story had ended differently than I'd expected. All along I'd been wondering, when is he going to get bitten? For when I had met Alex for the first time just a week ago, I had known only one fact about him: that he had once been bitten by a black mamba and survived. Had he left that out of the story then? All during our hike I'd been itching to ask him about this, but for some reason I couldn't. What had held me back? Perhaps just a fear of appearing too curious, too morbidly fascinated. Then again, he had probably told the story hundreds of times. Everyone acquainted with him seemed to know about it, and people liked to drop dark hints.

But now it was after midnight, and he was onto snakes. It was that time in North America (or anywhere in the world) when you either act sensibly and go straight to bed or else carry on as though sleep is something to be avoided at all costs and tomorrow might never come. So in the silence I looked over at Alex, his big face both shining and deeply shadowed in the firelight, and finally I said, "Isn't it true you were once bitten by a mamba?"

"You know about that?" he asked.

"Just by rumor . . ."

For a long time he gazed into the fire, the way a man does, as if tongues of flame were somehow capable of expressing the unutterable, mirroring the thoughts of the heart.

"It's a long story," he said eventually, "and it's not one I tell often anymore. Do you really want to hear it?"

I said I was all ears. The night was not just dark now, it was cold. That very day we had hiked through snow, along a high ridge, and though we had later descended into a valley there was still the crisp smell of nearby snow in the air. Somehow, even in such a setting, it did not seem the least bit extraordinary to be talking of African snakes. Alex put more logs on the fire while I went to the tent and got out our sleeping bags to wrap up in. And then he began.

"November," he said, "is a beautiful time in Zambia. It's my favorite time and place of all, anywhere on earth. The rains are just beginning, and after the long dry season the grass is coming up fresh and young and green. Everywhere the land is covered with flowers, the amazing wild flowers of Africa. All through the bush everything is enormously alive and singing. Even the animals seem filled with joy.

"Betty and I had been married just over a year, and we were stationed in Chizela where our mission had a small Bible school. Our life was so happy and peaceful it was almost like paradise. One afternoon I was out inspecting the grass on the airstrip, to see whether it needed to be cut for a supply plane that would be landing later that week. On the way back I began collecting a bouquet of flowers for Betty. I was wildly in love with her and still am. Well, I had wandered off the strip a short distance into the forest, where the grass was about calf-high, and soon I was on my way home with a good bunch of flowers. Then I saw one more—just one more flower, over there—a flame lily, a magnificent thing—it's the national flower of Zambia, you know—and I took two steps to reach for it when all at once, out of nowhere . . ."

But right here Alex was interrupted by one of those tremendous cracks, just like a rifle shot, exploding from the fire and spewing coals and showers of sparks almost as far as the tent, and for a few moments the two of us went hopping and scurrying around grinding out embers with the soles of our boots. Not until we were settled again did Alex continue.

"Well, it was just like that!" He laughed. "It was that unexpected. In Africa they speak of a man having 'snake eyes,' which means the ability to see snakes, to pick them out in the grass or bush. It's an acquired knack, and it's something I thought I had. So without being dreadfully worried about it, the fact is that I was being very careful that day. I really was watching like a hawk.

"In fact, I ought to make a digression here, and tell you what had happened to me just a week prior to this. Years had passed since my first encounter with the mamba, and in all that time I'd never seen another one. Many people live their entire lives in Africa without seeing a mamba at all, save in captivity. 'Snake parks,' as they're called, are very popular over there, and you see them everywhere. But to sight a mamba out in the wild is rare. One day, however, I was driving with a young student named Yoano along the road to Kalengwa, on a visit to the copper mine there. It was shortly after the death—or should I say the assassination?—of Dag Hammarskjold. You recall it was in northern Zambia that his plane crashed? That mystery has never been solved. But in many ways it was a period of great unrest for Zambia. Independence was in the wind, great matters of history hung in the balance, and how easily that balance could have tipped the wrong way! It is the tragedy of modern Africa that in most of the countries that is exactly what has happened.

"In any event it was a hot bright day and we were on our way to Kalengwa in a Land Rover when there in front of us, stretched out right across the road sunning himself, was a black mamba. He was a medium-sized fellow, about seven or eight feet long, and as soon as we realized what he was I gunned the motor and ran him over. In Africa you always kill a poisonous snake if you have the chance. But as I looked in the rearview mirror I saw this one still moving, crawling off slowly towards the bush.

"Well, just a few miles further on what do you think happened? We saw another mamba! And this one was an immense size, easily twelve feet long—a beautiful specimen—and there he was lying in the road with his long skin shining gun-metal gray. Once again I gunned the motor and headed straight for him, but this time, just as we were almost on top of the thing, he reared up on his tail to his full height and hovered there right in front of the windshield, ready to strike, so tall he towered over the roof of the Land Rover. What a monster he was! I'm telling you, we were scared stiff. Not that there was any real danger, for all the windows were done up tight—even though it was stifling hot, there were still the tsetse flies to worry about. Yet Yoano and I were both so shocked that we actually crashed our heads together trying to crouch down out of the way. And then when that mamba struck with all his force right into the center of the windshield, it was just like a bat out of hell. What an incredible experience! We were safe inside the cab, though, and we ran him over, and again as I looked back I saw the thing moving off slowly into the bush. But it was clear he wasn't feeling too well, and as for the two of us, we felt big bumps forming on our foreheads. It was so funny we burst out laughing—really a raucous, nerve-wracked sort of laughter, a release of hysteria. For there was nothing to be afraid of, and yet we had been terrified. And even as I laughed I was remembering my battle with the mamba from years before, and seeing again those frightful fangs, the black-lined mouth, the coffin-shaped head, and all the pure unleashed fury of darkness. How glad I was to be a Christian and to know that I was in the hands of a loving God. Even so, at that very moment I had a vague intimation that somehow I was not yet finished with this sinister creature, nor he with me. This was almost like an omen, a prophecy. But of course I immediately suppressed it, dismissed it as superstition.

"So all in all, it was a very eventful drive we had that day. In Africa you never know what is going to happen. After not seeing a mamba for years, I'd now seen two of them within an hour. It was very unusual, especially to spot a full-grown one. But this was just the beginning.

"Eventually we arrived at Kalengwa, about forty-five miles from Chizela, where we were to talk over plans for a mission among the miners. They have the richest copper mine in the world there, you know. Other places are happy with deposits of 2 percent or so, but at Kalengwa the ore is 87 percent pure. Incredible! And they found it just inches below the surface. For centuries men had walked right over it, unknowing.

"Well, Yoano and I went straight to the main office, but as soon as we stepped through the door what do you think we saw? That's right, a black mamba. Fortunately this one was in a cage, actually one of those big boxes Africans use for storing vegetables, made of fine mesh to keep the insects out. The man we were to meet with had been detained, but another fellow was there, and he was busy feeding the mamba with white mice. We stood around and watched as a live mouse was dropped into the cage. Immediately the mamba darted, sank in its fangs, and quickly withdrew. Within minutes paralysis set in. The little white face froze in a look of horror.

"So, I thought, once again I encounter my old friend. I had now seen three mambas in the same day, and each time our acquaintance was growing a little more intimate. I felt the way one might feel upon being in the same room with a famous person, yet someone who had achieved his fame in some hideous or unsavory manner. I couldn't tear myself away from the cage. Now the mamba was lathering the paralyzed body with saliva before swallowing it. For the longest time I watched, fascinated, until I realized that the snake's keeper was watching me.

"'I see you have a great interest in the mamba,' he said slowly. I can still hear the tone of his voice. It was just as if he had said something entirely different to me, such as, 'I can get you a prostitute if you want one.'

"After that I backed away from the cage. But on top of a desk in one corner I noticed a pile of books and articles about snakes. There was a lot of material on Ionides, the legendary snakehandler, whom I had met once. But what particularly caught my eye was an essay all about the habits of the black mamba. Since we had some time on our hands I sat down and read through it. It was a very strange piece of writing, full of the most precise and intimate data, even down to mating behaviour and the care of the young, yet written up not in our Western scientific fashion but more as a sort of mystical treatise. It was loaded with information that I wondered how it would be possible for a human being to discover, so that I concluded either the author knew exactly what he was talking about, or else it was total rubbish. One thing he said, for ex-

ample—and this was the part that especially intrigued me—
was that when the mamba strikes a human victim he always
strikes at the level of the grass. If the grass is ankle deep, he'll
get a man in the ankle; hip high, and he'll go for the hip.
Immediately after the strike he'll race away at a terrific speed,
traveling head up, with such a small part of his body touching
the ground that he may appear to be actually flying along the
top of the grass. Then at a distance of some twenty to twenty-
five yards away he'll stop dead, turn and face his victim, and
with head held high like a periscope he'll begin to wave,
swaying slowly, eerily, from side to side. And that wave: that's
the sign that he's coming back. He'll wait for a few minutes,
and then he'll come streaking back like lightning and strike
again for the final kill.

"Well, that's the sort of stuff that was in this article. I remember I read it almost in a trance. It was one of those cases—this happens to me too while reading the Bible—in which
every sentence seems to burn itself into the mind. And the
very last thing it said was that you can always recognize a
mamba victim, because the mamba takes out the eyes. In a
large animal that's all it will touch, only the eyes. And that's
the way this article ended.

"The very moment I finished reading, in walked the man we
had come to meet. He had some others with him and we sat
down to visit and pray together, and over the course of the
meeting I all but forgot about the snake. But I had seen three
black mambas that day, and whereas years before I had tangled with one face to face, now, after reading this amazing article, I felt strangely as if the creature himself had spoken to
me, whispered things in my ear.

"It was just a week later that I was out picking wild flowers
beside the airstrip in Chizela, as I've told you. Yet even with
all of this in the back of my mind, it came as a complete surprise when, just as I was reaching for this one last flower, this
flame lily, all at once I felt something slam into the back of my
leg. It was a real hit, like a gunshot, a powerful stinging blow

that actually made me jump into the air. I spun 'round, caught just a glimpse of the familiar coffin-shaped head and those eyes like the tiniest black diamonds, and knew immediately I was as good as dead. There had been no warning whatsoever, and yet instantly my astonishment gave way to an eerie sense of fatalism, as though I knew that everything had been meticulously and uncannily prepared for this very event. Is that, I wonder, what passes through everyone's mind at the moment of death? And I had another odd thought: she was a good size, this mamba, ten feet or so, and she struck me as being the spitting image of the one I'd killed in the hut, just like a twin sister, so that in that fleeting moment when I first laid eyes on her, I remember feeling that she knew exactly who I was. Crazy, isn't it? The fact is, she didn't know me from Adam, and probably I had simply made the mistake of venturing too near to her nest.

"That's how I know, by the way, that this one must have been a female, a mother, for in spite of all the legends, there is really only one situation in which a mamba will actually attack a human being out of the blue like that, and that is when the eggs are being threatened. So that's what I must have done, in reaching for one last flower.

"Well, I dropped that bouquet as if it were poison and stared in spellbound horror as the mamba went streaking away across the top of the grass, head up, swift and legless as a ghost. The grass was calf high, and sure enough, I'd been hit in the calf. You can imagine what I was thinking: the entire contents of that bizarre article were flashing through my mind. Exactly what the writer had described was happening to me now, just as though I'd dreamed it all. And then there came that final sign, that thing that even now sends a shudder through me just to think of it: the mamba had stopped about twenty-five yards away, and she was waving at me. Slowly, musically, telling me she was coming back. As if merely to kill once were not enough.

"As I say, I knew already I was a dead man. The mamba bite is always fatal. I had maybe eight minutes, twenty at the outside. Yet at the same time I thought—if I have to die, all right, but there's sure no reason I have to die *here*. Right beside me, as it happened, there was a huge tree—a *mukuyu*, I think, the African fig—and one other fact I had recalled from this article was that mambas have very poor eyesight. So the first thing I did was to hobble around behind this tree. Can you imagine? Hiding from a snake behind a tree? But that is what I did. And it gave me time to take out a handkerchief and tie a tourniquet on my leg, just below the knee. It was a beautiful tourniquet, I must say, right over the vessel. Isn't it peculiar how a little thing like that, at such a time, can give a fellow such deep satisfaction?

"Next I peered cautiously out from behind the trunk, just as in a game of cops and robbers, and saw that the mamba was still there, still waving. But now I was confident she couldn't see me. And so, keeping that big old friendly fig between me and the snake, I started edging away, backing off towards the airstrip, until I was out of the woods and figured it was safe— if anywhere at all was safe at that point. Then I took off like the dickens, straight up the runway for home, hopping on one leg all the way. It was utterly crazy—I shouldn't even have been moving, let alone running—but that's how I did it, and I went at a fierce clip. I'll bet I ran faster on one leg that day than I ever have on two! And so many thoughts were in my mind, I cannot tell them all. But I wanted to see Betty, for one thing. And I wanted to die in my own home and not on top of some mamba's lair. And I certainly didn't want my eyes chewed out!

"Yet there was one idea, strangely enough, that never occurred to me, not even for a moment. And that was the thought that I might survive, that the Lord might save me. I cried out to God with all my heart, naturally. But only because death already had me. I tore down that runway like a man who had one final act to perform in this world, and then the struggle would be over.

"Even before I got to the house I could feel the paralysis setting in. I think I must have taken the last couple of bounds with my legs nearly limp. But finally I crashed against the door and fell inside, yelling out to Betty that I'd been bitten by a black mamba. She gasped, and for a moment it looked as though she too might be paralyzed. But instantly she collected her wits and was all efficiency. She lanced the wound and sucked it out, for whatever that was worth, and I noticed that her hands weren't even trembling. She is a nurse, you know, and she did everything it was possible to do. We had a single vial of tropical serum on hand, which isn't at all effective against mamba, but she gave it to me anyway. This was before the days when there was any such thing as mamba antivenin, so that even if we'd been near a hospital it would have been game over. And still today mamba serum is so potent it's rarely administered. In any case Betty gave me three injections of this other stuff: one in the leg, one in the hip, and one in the shoulder. And then she gave me a heart stimulant and fussed around with some other things—I forget what all—but we both knew that none of it could really help. Finally I just lay there in her arms, and all she could do was listen to me describe the progress of the paralysis: now it was up to my waist, now my stomach, now my chest went out, and so on.

"At about this point one of the Bible-school students came in—this same Yoano with whom I'd traveled to Kalengwa the week before. He was only a boy, in his late teens, but he was very sharp and we liked him enormously. He took one look at me and asked what was wrong, and as soon as I said 'mamba' I saw his eyes go wide, big as saucers. It was fear, you know. And I could see it like immense, fathomless caves in his eyes. I'll never forget that. So I looked back and forth between Betty's eyes, which were a bit calmer, and this boy's, because when you are dying you do not look at anything but people's eyes, and that is what they look at in you. After all, this is it. It's the hour of truth.

"But all at once as I looked at Yoano, I saw his eyes get small again, and I realized there was something new in his face. And that's when he said to me, 'Mamba is great, bwana. Very powerful. That is true. But it is also true that we have a great God, a God mightier than any snake. And we will pray for you.'

"*Pray for me!* Though I'd been praying all my life, it seemed such a novel thought. And this was the student talking to his principal! Yet for me it was the first glimmer of hope. Before this I hadn't had an ounce of faith. The mamba always killed, and quickly. Why should it be any different for me than for others? The Lord may keep a man's foot from falling, but when the foot has already slipped, then it's too late. Isn't it? Will God reach out and save a man when he's already fallen off the cliff? Will He send a band of angels to bear him up? The story of Paul being bitten by the viper never crossed my mind. But I saw that boy's eyes go suddenly small again and heard him say they would pray, and faith jumped in me like a live nerve. I kept on with the countdown—the paralysis was up to my shoulders now, now at my neck, now in the back of my throat—and the last thing I remember was trying to tell them that I couldn't talk, but no words would come. And then the lights went out.

"It's a beautiful way to die really. No pain at all, just slowly going to sleep. Such a death is much more painful for the person who watches than for the one who experiences it. And Betty was eight months pregnant with our first child. Yes!

"Later she told me that right after I lost consciousness she rushed out of the house to get some more medication from the clinic. She knew it was hopeless, but that doesn't mean you give up. On the way all she could think of was that the baby in her womb would never see his father. For her that was the worst part of it. And on top of everything else, she had felt contractions coming on all that morning.

"Meanwhile Yoano had hold of my limp hand and was praying for me, while somebody else ran to the schoolhouse and rang the bell, the one we used for classes and for chapel and also to signal emergencies. In no time at all a great prayer meeting was underway outside our little house, and as the hours dragged on the students took turns praying over me in small groups. Living hands held onto me continuously, and in one way or another the whole community was mobilized to keep life inside a body that normally ought to have been given up for dead. In the middle of all this a messenger arrived from one of the villages to say that a woman was in labor, and could Betty please come? Of course Betty had to say no—she was in labor herself! It was a crazy, crazy time. Yet isn't it amazing how new life can come bursting forth right on the heels of death?

"The closest hospital was at Mukinge, a hundred miles away, and a doctor was radioed from there, more for Betty's sake than for mine. When he arrived he checked me over, but there was really nothing to be done. He just shook his head and said, 'He's still ticking, that's all I know,' and then he spent the next few hours attending to Betty, setting things up as best he could for a premature delivery. Meanwhile the prayer meeting carried on, and at Mukinge too they were praying, and all the other mission stations were notified as well.

"Sometime after midnight—about the same hour it is now— the doc poked his head in to check on me. Taking hold of my hand to feel the pulse, he thought for a moment it was gone, but just then my eyelids flickered open. I don't know which one of us was the more astounded. As for me—and I know it sounds trite to say this—I seriously wondered whether we were both in Heaven! He was a dear friend, and I just gawked at him and he at me. And I saw his eyes go wide, just like Yoano's. Only this time I knew it was the wideness of joy.

"'Alex,' he whispered to me, 'you have a baby boy.'

"I was delirious! I had a splitting headache, but at the same time I felt like jumping up and shouting and dancing. Of course I still couldn't move a muscle, and I was far from being out of the woods. But it was absolutely incredible the way all of these events meshed together. Sometimes the Lord seems to delight in filling us with every conceivable emotion at once, as if just to prove how much a man can hold. Later Betty tried to tell me what it was like to be in labor while grieving for her husband. She had tried to pray, but really she thought I was a goner, and she was having a terrible time accepting it. It was only as she sat up and held our new son in her arms that she was able to say to the Lord, 'All right, all right. Now You can take Alex. Now You can have him.' And seconds later I was waking up!

"Well, I won't go into all the details of my recovery. But over the course of that night the feeling gradually came back into my body, as if I were being unfrozen, until by morning I had movement everywhere but in my legs. They shipped me over to Mukinge Hospital, where for two days longer the legs remained paralyzed, so that they were worried I might never walk again. There was also terrible chest pain, headache, and nausea, and I wasn't able to urinate. But on the third day I felt a muscle quiver in my calf: it was exactly the place where the mamba had hit me, only on the opposite leg. And then for a while those two legs of mine jumped and vibrated all over the place, just like a bagful of snakes, as the expression goes. People were making great jokes about it, saying, for example, how Alex must be getting filled with the Holy Spirit. And who knows, maybe that's exactly what was happening.

"In any case three weeks later I was out of the hospital, walking around, pushing my son in a pram, wrapping Christmas presents, and all in all looking at the world through brand new eyes. For such an experience has the effect of renewing a man, washing him so clean that he has to get used to himself all over again. We Christians say we are 'born again,' you know. But it's been my experience that this phenomenon of new birth, of knowing oneself alive in a brand new way, is something that comes to a believer over and over again. God's purposes for us are so unlimited.

"The same day I was released from the hospital, incidentally, I was out walking in the garden when I caught sight of a snake, and just about jumped out of my skin. He was only a

tiny harmless thing, more like a little worm, but still he gave
me a good start, and I felt so sheepish. But do you know, after that one incident I have never again been afraid of a snake.
And how well I recall the first time I came across another
black mamba. My initial reaction was one of pure hatred: All I
wanted to do was to get him. Silly, isn't it? The vindictiveness,
the instinct for vengeance. Just like Captain Ahab and Moby
Dick. But that too passed, and ever since then I have been
completely freed from any of the natural jitters most people
have in regard to snakes. I would almost say that I feel inocu-
lated against them, so that just as Daniel went into the lions'
den, I sometimes imagine I could walk into any snake pit
without a qualm. Not that I'm boasting—just telling you a
mystery. What it is, of course, is the simple confidence I have
that my life is nothing but a pure gift from the Lord, and that
He will take me to Himself at exactly the right time, in the
way He ordains, no later and no sooner.

"One other result of my brush with the mamba is that it has
given me a peculiar closeness to black Africans. It's curious,
but when they know the story their attitude toward me
changes, in a way so subtle it is impossible to describe. But
many treat me almost as one of themselves. Because, they'll
say, 'You've tasted the poison of Africa.'

"'Yes,' I sometimes reply, 'And God tasted the poison of the
whole world when He hung on the cross.'"

For a long time now we had not put any more wood on the
fire. There were no flames, just coals glowing like a heap of
jack-o-lanterns, a pile of little skulls lit from inside. I had not
noticed, but at some point the clouds had rolled away, and
now above us, visible through the black lace of the tree
branches, there were stars, like diamond-headed nails. I had
thought that Alex was finished, but after a while he added
something else.

"Some years later, with my three sons, I was visiting a zoo
in South Africa and we were standing by a cage looking in at
the black mamba. I was telling the kids, 'I was bitten by one

of those,' when the man beside us turned around and said, most vehemently, 'Oh, no you weren't!'

"'Oh, yes I was,' I stated bluntly.

"'If you'd been bitten by one of those,' he insisted, 'you wouldn't be here.'

"As it turned out, this fellow was a herpetologist who was in the process of compiling a book all about the black mamba. He also happened to be the son of one of the world's top authorities on snakes.

"'All right,' he said finally. 'You tell me exactly what happened to you, and then I'll tell you whether or not you were bitten by a black mamba.' He was aware, you see, that very few people really know snakes. Especially in a place like Africa, which teems with different varieties, correct identification is always precarious. So I told him the story—how the snake struck at calf level, went zooming off, stopped and waved, and so on—and when I was finished he just bowed his head and mumbled, 'Yup, that was the mamba, all right.' He'd never heard of anyone surviving a bite.

"Well, what a priceless opportunity this was for a professional missionary! For the next hour or so we sat together on the grass in front of the mamba cage—right under the nose of Satan, I like to think!—while I told this highly educated man, this scientist, all about the power and the love of Christ. And similar chances have come to me countless times over the years, for even though the Bible is full of stories such as mine, people always seem amazed to hear that God, in this day and age, is real, real enough to rescue a man even out of the jaws of death. But I ask them, 'If He cannot save in this life, how will He ever save in the next?'"

Once again Alex stopped, and the silence between us grew so long this time that I began to be quite uneasy. There is an odd way in which a good story will reveal as much in the person who hears as in the person who tells. And though I'd hardly said a word all night, it seemed just by the way I'd listened that I'd given myself away. There was little doubt in my mind that God, if He was any sort of God at all, had the power to save a man from the bite of the mamba, and even to close the mouths of lions if He wanted to. But the real issue was, did He want to? Not *could* He, but *would* He?

A thousand such questions jostled inside me, none of which I dared to voice. Merely to open my mouth, it seemed, would be to doubt the existence of love itself.

"Alex?" I said finally. "I know that more things are wrought by prayer than this world knows. But how sure are you that it was prayer that saved you? I mean, that it wasn't just some freak?"

"As sure as I'm sitting here," he answered. And it wasn't only prayer, my friend. It was the Lord. Let's go to bed."

Fact and Fiction

By weighing, studying, and setting in order many proverbs, the Teacher imparted his knowledge to the people. He labored to find just the right words, and the things he wrote were upright and true.

—ECCLESIASTES 12:9–10

I like to picture Jesus in the act of creating His parables: lying out on a green hillside hour after hour, chewing on a straw, leaning back on His elbows with the clouds drifting by overhead like sheep, and polishing and polishing every sentence of His stories, knowing full well how very much could depend upon a single word, a single turn of phrase.

A fanciful scene? Perhaps. But really there is no way of knowing which of Jesus' ideas may have come to Him full-blown from the mind of His Father, in flashes of Holy-Spirited inspiration, or to what extent He might have had to plane and hammer them out just as He had planed and hammered boards in His earthly father's carpentry shop. Perhaps the best we can do is to cite the experience of Ecclesiastes, who "labored to find just the right words." Such labor, we can only presume, would have been necessary even for God's Son.

Creating a good story can be something like planning a romantic candlelit dinner just for two, with lace tablecloth, good wine, the best silver, perhaps a violin in the background, and a table that is exactly the right size to allow for a chance brushing of fingers across it or a touching of ankles beneath. And of course all this must be shared with precisely the right person, and the setting and timing must be perfect. Everything must be just so, for the least impropriety could spell the difference between kindling the fire of love or dousing the whole affair with a pail of cold water. Such painstaking attention to the tiniest details may not be so important for an old married couple, but between a man and a woman who are not yet intimate everything can hang upon the inflection of a syllable. And of course the fundamental reason for writing stories is (or should be) the kindling of love.

So I like to think about Jesus the artist, brooding prayerfully over His creations in much the way I have done over these stories of mine. For prayer, essentially, *is* creation; it is participation in the ongoing creative work of the Father. Very often it is a matter of knowing *just the right words* to speak in order to bring whole new worlds into existence. And not just the right words but the right images, the right concepts, the right forms and genres. As Jesus put it in John 12:49, "I did not speak on My Own initiative, but the Father who sent Me instructed Me what to say, and *also how to say it.*"

As a writer of fiction I ponder much upon the "how" of Jesus' storytelling. And I also ponder the "where." Where did He get His story ideas? Oh, I know Who it was Who inspired Him. But what was His raw material? Even the Creator, after all, when He fashioned man, stooped to using a lump of clay. So I wonder, for example, what might have been the seed image behind the parable of the prodigal son?

Was Jesus reclining at supper one night, perhaps somewhere in the vicinity of His old home town of Nazareth, when one of His disciples happened to remark to Him, "Say, Master do you remember that fellow you grew up with—the one who ran away from home and squandered his entire inheritance down in Egypt? Well, guess what? He's come back. Yeah, that's right. Crawling on his knees too. And you should have seen that sourpuss older brother of his when Dad slaughtered the fattened calf. Was he ever mad!"

Well, this is pure conjecture. But the point is that while the parables of Jesus certainly fall into the category of "fiction," it is also fairly certain that some sort of factual raw material would have lain behind many of them. And some of the stories must have had a greater basis in fact than others. In Luke 13, for example, we see Jesus making parabolic application of two current news stories: the collapse of a tower in Siloam, and Pilate's sadistic use of human blood (and Galilean blood at that) in some atrocious mockery of a religious ceremony. Jesus, it seems, employed whatever material came to hand, and so it is tempting to speculate about the source of such a strange story as the parable of the dishonest steward in Luke 16. Had the Master perhaps heard tell of a case just like this? And did He in fact marvel at the clever, self-possessed manner in which this fellow had handled the collapse of his career? Is it even possible that this same unemployed steward had gone on to become one of Christ's disciples, so that all those in the inner circle would have known perfectly well that the story alluded to a factual situation?

Whatever the case, can we go so far as to guess, perhaps, that there were times in Jesus' stories when even the Lord's contemporaries would have had difficulty knowing for sure (much as we do with many modern novels) just where the facts ended and the fiction began?

In the case of "Mamba," the first story in this book, the events related happen to contain much more fact than fiction. Never will I forget the night when Roy Comrie, a veteran missionary with Africa Evangelical Fellowship (AEF), sat in our living room and for upwards of an hour held us spellbound with his firsthand account of being bitten by a black mamba and surviving to tell the tale. Similarly it was at a missions conference that I first heard guest speaker Bob Foster, also a missionary with AEF, spin his true spine-tingling yarn about wrestling eyeball-to-eyeball with a black mamba in a little thatched hut somewhere out in the wilds of Zambia.

People such as Bob Foster and Roy Comrie, I have come to learn, live and breathe an atmosphere of true-life stories. In their day-to-day work they live the sort of stories that the Bible itself bristles with, and then they breathe out those tales by retelling them with real bardic flair and mastery. In fact, a good deal of their teaching and preaching ministry (together with their personal witnessing) consists of passing on the amazing firsthand accounts of the Lord's wonderful workings in their own lives and in the work of their mission. Often enough they are content simply to let such stories speak for themselves. They know that evangelism isn't a matter of twisting arms and making oneself a pest, but rather of "holding out the word of life" (Phil. 2:16) in such a way as to make the truth of Christ incarnate, in deed as well as in word, for an unbelieving world.

In committing to literary form the factual experiences of these two men with the black mamba I have obviously taken considerable artistic liberties. Not least of these was the decision to combine the two narratives into one, as though all the events had happened to a single person. Furthermore the portrait of that one character, the fictional missionary named Alex, is not intended to be a portrait of either Bob Foster or Roy Comrie. Even the narrator does not correspond to myself; rather, he's a person standing on the very edge of the Christian faith and peering in (trying perhaps to find some reason good enough to believe). Beyond this the source material has been tampered with in a number of more minor ways: by the addition of new thoughts here and there, the enhancing of symbolism, the fine tuning of the language, the juggling of a few plot details, and so on. Yet I hasten to add that none of these artistic changes has been such as to seriously alter the essential truth of the original stories. The facts have been molded for dramatic purposes, but not exaggerated.

Yet why, it might be asked, if these stories were so good in the first place, have I bothered to change them at all? It is one thing to tell the tale in my own words, highlighting certain points, but why go to all the trouble of actually fictionalizing this material, casting and recasting every phrase and image? Well, my only excuse is that I am a writer of fiction, a person possessed of a mind that works naturally (and to some extent, I trust, supernaturally) along those lines. And when I hear the Lord's great commission to "go into all the world and preach the gospel," personally what I tend to hear is this: "Go into the world of fiction and preach the gospel there too. And preach it in the language of the natives, which is the artistic language of literature."

The Changeling

A miracle is like a murder mystery. Everyone has their own theory as to how it happened and who done it. All you can say for sure is that the most obvious explanation can probably be ruled out, if only on the grounds that it does not make for a very good story.

It was Christmas Eve and Joe Szloboda finished his bacon and eggs and coffee and put on his duffle coat to walk down to work. Outside, huge snowflakes the size of rose petals were drifting down out of the black, peaceful night. Joe stopped to look at them in wonder. Then he tilted back his head, opened his mouth wide, and stood there, deliberately waiting for one of the big wet flakes to land on his tongue. He didn't have to wait long, and tasting the little cold fallen star, he whispered, "H-H-Holy J-Jesus, m-m-m-may all c-creation b-b-bless you this n-n-night!"

Most people couldn't understand a word Joe Szloboda said. He stuttered horrendously, and besides that, whenever he spoke to anyone, he had a habit of looking down at his feet and mumbling so softly as to be almost inaudible. In his youth the problem had driven him nearly crazy with embarrassment and frustration, and in one way or another all of his life's dreams had been dashed.

For the past several years, however, he had held a job as a night janitor at a small department store. He slept most of the day, ate breakfast just as the rest of the world was sitting down to supper, and then worked in the store from closing time until the wee hours of the morning. The schedule had been hard to adapt to at first, but after a tortured and chaotic

youth this strange new rhythm had gradually introduced a
marvelous order and calm into Joe's existence, so that at thir-
ty-five he now enjoyed more stability and happiness than at
any other period in his life. Though he still suffered from in-
tense loneliness it was nevertheless true that Joe Szloboda,
without having at all planned it, had somehow stuttered his
way into a life of extraordinary peace and interior joy.

In recent years he had developed a habit of arriving at the
store about an hour before work. During this time he liked to
sit down in the furnace room, where he was sure of not being
disturbed, and read his Bible. This was the place where he
had first discovered how to pray, in the middle of many a
lonely night when he was so depressed that he could not find
the strength or the heart to sweep one more square foot of
floor. At such times he would come down here, sit on a three-
legged stool, and talk to the warm, humming darkness. Here
he could hold his head up and speak eye to eye. There was
the faintest dancing glow from inside the furnace. Though he
stuttered as thickly as ever he knew his prayers were compre-
hended. Even short prayers gave him not only physical
strength to carry on with his work but peace and a light
heart.

So instead of taking coffee breaks Joe learned to use his free
time for devotions—not because of any burden of guilt or
duty but solely out of a love for the one who came to meet
him in the night. He would read and pray; work; pray again;
go back to work; then read and pray some more. Even the
work itself began to take on an attitude of prayer, and in time
his whole shift at the store grew to be infused with the sort of
deep life of continuous contemplation that is sometimes discovered by those driven into solitude. Without being in the
least aware of it Joe Szloboda had begun to live the life of a
monk.

It was still snowing when he arrived at the store. Standing
for a moment at the back door, in the laneway, he watched the
big flakes falling like tufts of wool out of the vast night and

making the most perfect landings on hydro wires, on fence-posts, on window sills, and on one black cat huddled among the garbage cans. The singing of a group of carollers floated over from somewhere across the lane. Joe caught another snowflake on his tongue and thanked Jesus for it. It was better than any present that could be bought in the store that he would be spending his Christmas Eve cleaning (though of course this thought never crossed his mind).

Inside the building Joe paused again and said, or rather thought, another short prayer. He wanted everything he did in the store to be a sacrifice to Christ. Often as he went down the stairs into the furnace room he experienced a palpable wave of relief, of homecoming. In his tiny apartment he slept and ate and it was always noisy. But here he worked and he prayed. The store at night was as still as any church. The basement room was warm and plain and dark and the aura of it welcomed and embraced him like a presence, a friend, almost like the wife he had never had.

His Bible he kept in a small orange crate beneath the stairs, wrapped in a velvet cloth. Also in the box was a wooden cross, which he had carved himself, and a candle. He always read very slowly, and because he looked through and beyond the page more than at it he liked to read by candlelight. To-night this seemed especially appropriate, and spreading the velvet cloth over the crate, he set the cross on it, lit the candle, and opened his Bible to a portion of the Christmas story in Luke. When he came to the account of the shepherds with the words, "And the glory of the Lord shone round about them," Joe paused and said the verse over and over, out loud, stuttering as usual. Sometimes when he did this, it would almost seem as though his impediment became a little less noticeable; but perhaps it was just that he himself was less conscious of it. Certainly there was something wonderfully quiet about the words of the Lord, deep and calming. They were like snowflakes that had been falling and falling forever through supernal space and were finally coming to settle with exquisite gentleness in the pit of one human heart. Eventually Joe knelt on the cement floor beside the orange-crate altar and prayed, his one candle burning almost audibly and the furnace glowing, as outside the whole great night filled up with the infinite white of Christmas.

By the time Joe made his appearance upstairs the rest of the staff would normally have gone home, and he would have the building all to himself. Again, there was an extraordinary sense of Presence hovering over Joe's shoulder here, inhabiting the deserted aisles and all night long rushing up and down the great empty stairway in the middle of the store. Joe couldn't really explain it. He knew that his inability to cope with the speech problem had turned him into a peculiarly isolated man, as lonely as could be. But he also knew that he never felt really alone anymore.

During the Christmas season the first thing he liked to do on his shift was to go to the front of the store and inspect the nativity scene that was set up there. It was just inside the big set of revolving doors that opened onto the street, and often careless shoppers would have tossed scraps of paper and other litter among the figures of Mary and Joseph, the animals, the wise men and shepherds. Once Joe had found a pop can in the cradle. So he liked to clean these things out and dust off the figures. It was a way of reminding himself that whatever work he might engage in, his real task was to do everything as if for the Lord Himself, to be a caretaker in the house of his God.

Tonight he stood before the stable scene and thought of this, of the Lord's first earthly home. This night in particular the scene in front of him with its life-sized characters began to seem so vivid that he might have been there himself, just one more of the humble figures gathered around the cradle in Bethlehem, adoring. To have leapt back over two thousand years, and yet to be in the eternal present, in the presence of Eternity Himself—this was an indescribable sensation, passing understanding. Yet all at once an even stranger sensation came on top of this one, and Joe actually put his hand up to his hair because there seemed to be static electricity coming out of it, effervescing all over his head. At the same time his attention was diverted by something in the creche, something that appeared different about it, that he couldn't quite put a finger on. What was it? His entire body tingled now with expectation, vibrant as a thrummed chord. And then Joe's mouth fell open in astonishment.

"Jesus!" he whispered.

And then, "O my precious Lord!"

And just as if his own name were being called out Joe Szloboda stepped forward and walked right into the center of the creche and knelt down beside the cradle. Joy was welling up inside him, a great bolt of pure, bounding joy, energetic and muscular like a huge fish leaping out of the water into sunlight. For as Joe gazed into the cradle he knew beyond any doubt that what he was seeing there was *real*. It was the incarnation of God and he was seeing it with his own eyes and it was real. There was no question of *how* real it was, or *what sort* of real, or whether such reality might have some psychological explanation.

Oh, no! People who have seen Jesus do not worry their heads over such things.

For what Joe Szloboda was seeing in that cradle was not the painted plaster infant with the golden halo that he had lovingly dusted so many times. No. What he saw, rather, was a *live baby*, a tiny breath of pink flesh who couldn't have been more than a few hours old. While the plaster Christ had sat up boldly and fixed the world with a thoroughly adult gaze from amid its straightjacket of swaddling bands, this living infant whom Joe now beheld, this little human rosebud of ineffable wonder, was bare naked and sound asleep.

Joe Szloboda, naturally, did not know the first thing about babies. But that did not impede the great current of love that was racing all through him like velvet lightning, and it did not stop him from throwing aside all reservations regarding his own clumsiness and all questions of religious protocol to reach out and gather up the helpless infant into his arms. After all, this baby needed mothering, and Joe was there to give it. None of the other figures had come alive, he observed; even Mary looked on cold and unmoved, statue that she was. And so, wrapping the live Holy Child in his own flannel shirt, Joe knelt there in the synthetic straw amid the staring crowd of plaster witnesses and was perfectly enraptured with the baby Jesus warm and still asleep and astoundingly light in his arms.

Just then Joe heard a sound at the front of the building and looked up to see Mr. Frank Thomas, the store manager, jangling a bunch of keys as he came in through one of the big glass doors. The first thing this man saw, of course, and could not help but see, was his janitor kneeling beside the crib in the manger scene, with head bowed, so that inevitably the unwelcome thought crossed his mind: *The fellow was praying.*

Now catching a man at prayer was like catching him without his clothes on, and naturally Thomas wondered what to say or whether he should say anything at all. Joe Szloboda, for his part, was too rooted in bliss to be worried about how he must have appeared to the outside world or even to be very surprised that a representative of that world should be returning to the store at this hour on Christmas Eve. In any event, caught in this archetypal encounter between the ecstatic and the mundane, for longer than a moment the two men simply locked gazes.

Thomas knew that Szloboda was a strange character. When the new manager had first come to the store three years before, he had made a couple of heroic efforts to engage the stutterer in conversation. For cleaning personnel, as everyone knew, enjoyed considerable status among executives, and a smart businessman counted it a lucky honor if he could strike up a pleasant acquaintance with a janitor. But in the case of

Joe Szloboda, of course, this was impossible, and Thomas, like all the other employees in the store, had soon abandoned any attempt to get to know him. What with Joe's odd hours, his incomprehensible speech, and his excruciating shyness, it had actually been years since any colleague had exchanged more than a few words with him. Everyone, and especially Joe himself, had simply given up. He didn't even go to the staff parties. And as always happened in such cases people took it for granted that there was much more wrong with Joe than simply a mechanical speech impediment. When a man could not communicate with anyone, the safest bet was to assume that he was right off his rocker and had best be left alone.

Frank Thomas, therefore, stared uncomfortably at Joe Szloboda, and Joe, still overcome with awe, cradled the baby Jesus in his arms and gazed back. Finally Thomas broke into nervously jovial laughter and burst out, "Hello there, Joe. A merry Christmas to you!" But the janitor's mysterious expression did not change, nor did he make any reply, and Thomas, following another awkward pause, went on to explain that he had a couple of last-minute presents he wanted to pick up. "You know how husbands are when it comes to shopping," he said, giggling like a schoolgirl.

In order to get where he was going in the store Thomas had to walk right past the creche, within a few feet of the kneeling janitor. But as he proceeded to do so he couldn't help but become aware of the little bundle Joe seemed to be cradling in his arms. Until now Thomas had been in too much of a hurry and too preoccupied with his own thoughts to think of pausing for long, or even to take much notice of the fact that the man was stripped down to his undershirt. He appeared, sure enough, to be in an attitude of prayer, but then again, he might just have been kneeling down to clean something. So what of it?

But now Thomas was curious.

"Say, Joe, what've you got there? Is something wrong?"

It was a rhetorical question, more or less. Yet Joe answered it. Staring up at Thomas with probably the biggest eyes and the steadiest gaze the manager had ever seen in his life, he said to him in a tone somehow both bright and dark with wonder, "It's Jesus, Mr. Thomas. Don't you recognize Him? He's come again!"

Thomas gawked. Jesus? Come again? The words did not register. What did register, however, was the fact that the imbecilic Joe Szloboda had looked him straight in the eye and spoken to him, perfectly clearly and intelligibly. Indeed his voice carried a disarming measure of what might have been termed gravity, or even, perhaps, authority.

Once again, Thomas was at a loss for words. But the very first thought that occurred to him was this: that all these years this man had been making a fool of him and of everyone in the store. For the obvious fact was, he could speak as plainly as anybody! So what sort of game had he been playing? Right then and there Thomas's attitude hardened into suspicion, although at the same time he determined to act as if nothing the least bit unusual had occurred. He wasn't going to bat an eyelash. A game could be played by two.

Still, he was curious.

"Come on, Joe, what's going on here? What've you got there?"

Again Joe fixed him with a gaze of unnerving beatitude, and in a string of clear, unbroken English repeated that this was Jesus Christ, alive in his arms, that our Lord and Savior had come again.

This time Thomas heard what the janitor said. The words registered, and he didn't like them. He didn't like them one bit. In a flash the thought came to him—maybe this guy was a real lunatic and had finally gone right around the bend. The manager hesitated, wondering how to proceed. Simple propriety dictated that he should say something pleasant. But he wondered how polite it was necessary to be to a madman. Then Joe spoke again.

"Come and see, Mr. Thomas. Come and behold the Lord Jesus."

Instinctively, involuntarily, Thomas stepped forward. And looked. First he caught sight of the empty cradle. And then he peered into the nest of flannel shirt on Joe's lap.

And he saw just the face of a tiny, live baby.

"Hey! What's going on here?" he stammered, taking a step back. "Joe, where did that baby come from? What's it doing here?"

Joe repeated that this was the Holy Child, the Son of God—and didn't Mr. Thomas recognize Him?

The manager stood up straight and looked all around the store. He wanted just to leave this crazy man alone, to pick up his few things and go home to his family. But the sight of a live baby had brought a million questions to his mind. For one thing, he didn't like the thought of seeing this helpless infant in the hands of a man who could be utterly demented. Something here, he was beginning to fear, might be very, very wrong.

"Joe," he said earnestly, "where did you get that baby? Who is its mother?"

Joe pointed at the painted plaster figure of the Virgin Mary.

Thomas stroked his chin. The man obviously had a one-track mind. Either that, or he was deliberately stalling and acting dumb. Flustered, the manager wanted to get to the bottom of this thing quickly. Impatiently he peppered the janitor with questions. The answers came back, clear, grave, serene. Just to hear such a voice emerging from the lips of a man who had always let on that he was totally withdrawn and inarticulate—well, it was incredible. It was monstrous. But finally Thomas satisfied himself that he had pried out the plain facts, or at least, as much of them as he was going to get: that in stopping to clean the nativity scene Joe had discovered this real baby in place of the plaster doll. It was as simple as that.

Summoning every remaining ounce of his patience, Thomas now got down on his knees in front of Joe and the little bundle, and putting his two hands squarely on the janitor's shoulders, he spoke to him as coolly and seriously as he knew how.

"Joe, listen to me. This is very important. That baby is *not* Jesus. You've made a mistake. Do you understand? It's a mistake, and it's very important for you to realize that. This baby belongs to somebody, and we've got to find out who. Can you understand?"

Joe repeated, somewhat sadly this time, that he was very sorry Mr. Thomas did not know the Lord Jesus Christ. And at that Thomas flew off the handle.

"You stupid dimwit!" he cried. "That baby is no more Jesus than you are! Can't you get that through your thick skull? Some stupid little teenage whore had that kid in a back alley somewhere, and she's left the thing here to get rid of it. That's all there is to it. Can't you see that? And we have to figure out what to do with the blessed thing."

Thomas folded his arms and felt oddly satisfied, in an uncertain sort of way, with his little explosion. He was more in control of the situation now. Motioning to Joe, he ordered him firmly to bring the kid and follow him upstairs to his office. Joe obeyed, and the two men mounted the great flight of stairs in the center of the store, the janitor slightly behind and still cradling the strange, warm little bundle who, through it all, had remained fast asleep in his arms.

In the manager's office Frank Thomas sat in his black leather chair behind the oak desk and waved his employee into a straight chair in the corner. Then he reached for the telephone book and thumbed peremptorily through various listings. Although he was not quite certain which authority to notify in the case of an abandoned infant, long practice as a manager had taught him to appear, even to himself, as though he knew exactly what he was doing. Repeatedly his eye coasted over the phone number of the police, and yet he kept thinking—for a tiny baby? The cops? But finally he called them, giving a curt explanation, and then he sat back to await their arrival. It had been good, for a moment, just to talk to another human being, to hear the voice of a sane person. His inability to communicate with Joe and the eerie transformation in the latter's speech and manner had been telling on his nerves. But now, alone with this man, there was more time to be passed.

Beyond the window snow was sifting down in white, other-worldly silence. Absentmindedly Thomas studied it, and for a few seconds he fancied the scene resembled a deep skyful of stars, in motion against the dark glass. And thinking this, all at once he felt himself a boy again, lying out on the hillside at his stepfather's farm . . .

"Mr. Thomas, would you like to hold the baby Jesus?"

Joe's voice seemed to come to him from the other side of the universe. It caught the manager off guard, so that turning towards the man and the baby in the corner of his office, suddenly he saw them there as if for the first time. And if the truth be told, at that precise instant Thomas' heart nearly melted, as, heavy with a cosmic nostalgia, he was stabbed by the achingly beautiful picture: the tiny sleeping newborn, wrapped in plaid flannel, and lowly Joe Szloboda in his undershirt and green coveralls with his eyes shining and his big red hands buried in the warm bundle. They looked, the two of them, almost holy.

It was a strange event for a Christmas Eve.

There would be a few minutes yet before the police arrived. Perhaps he had been too hard on Joe, Thomas mused, too hasty. He considered asking the man pointblank about his stutter. Maybe there was more to this story than met the eye.

Just at that point, however, the buzzer rang at the front of the store, and abruptly the manager's mood changed as he hurried downstairs to usher in the police.

Yes, a miracle is like a murder mystery. Except that in the case of the miracle it is not always clear whether anything out of the ordinary has happened at all. The evidence, somehow, is never quite as compelling as the evidence of a dead body.

Frank Thomas led the police officers, a man and a woman, up to his office. With four adults present it seemed very crowded in the small room, and Thomas prattled away as though he, rather than the janitor, were the one most knowledgeable about the case. The fellow was a bit slow, he explained, and seemed to be under the delusion—here Thomas lowered his voice decorously—that the abandoned child was Jesus Christ. At this the officers raised their eyebrows and studied Joe most curiously.

Joe, for his part, said nothing. Even after his boss had run out of words the janitor sat perfectly still, gazing down at the baby and making no reply to any question. During these oddly cavernous silences the sound of the snow could actually be heard, the flakes batting like tiny paws against the windowpane. After a while the policewoman stepped forward and gently asked Joe to hand over the child to her. Reluctantly, but still without a word, the janitor surrendered his precious bundle.

Just then the baby woke up and began to cry. The men, out of their depth now, hung their heads or looked awkwardly about the room, while the woman rocked the child, cooed, walked him up and down, nestled him against her blue uniform and spoke ever so soothingly, yet all without being able to comfort him. At length the janitor broke his silence and, without a hint of accusation but in a voice unnaturally direct, almost parental, said, "Try holding him close to your heart." And at that the policewoman, accompanied by her colleague, removed the child from the room, leaving Frank Thomas and Joe Szloboda alone to listen to the plaintive sound of the crying as it receded down the stairway and into the distance, floating back up to them haltingly, chokingly, yet somehow with strange expressiveness, like a kind of nearly intelligible stuttering.

There descended then upon the two men the longest and most singularly pregnant of pauses, with the snow crashing loud as thunder against the dark panes of glass.

Mystery Fiction

I will open my mouth in parables,
I will utter mysteries hidden since the world's creation.

—PSALM 78:2

I remember hearing once about a reader who made a hobby out of collecting Christmas murder mysteries. Apparently there are scores of these, making this curious artifact something of a genre in its own right. And this, it seems to me, is entirely appropriate. For while the story of Christ begins innocently enough, in the lovely and touching scene of a newborn babe in a manger, at the end of the tale someone gets murdered, and that someone turns out to be the Son of God.

Someone is accountable for that death. Someone is guilty.

And someone is going to be found out.

Consider the evidence. There is a weapon—the cross. There is a bloodstain—the eucharistic wine. There is a dead body—the bread. There is a motive—sin. And there are murderers—you and I. And there is also a private eye assigned to the case, a super sleuth whose job it is to match the crime with the criminal, to tie all of the evidence together and clinch a conviction.

Thank God, the name of that master detective is Grace. Thank God, it is the Holy Spirit who not only tracks down the culprit, but pleads the case for the prosecution, and convicts us. Because the miracle of the gospel is this: that the moment of conviction is the moment of reprieve. And when our day in court arrives the one whom we ourselves have murdered shall stand before our very eyes in the witness box, alive once more, and reckon with us—a fact that by all rights ought to terrify the living daylights out of us. But instead, as we confess our guilt and admit the absolute justice of the prosecution's case, it is this very Paschal Victim Himself who finally turns to us and pronounces the astonishing verdict, *"Not Guilty!"*

And though our sins were as scarlet, suddenly they shall be white as snow.

Is it a foretaste of this event that transpires in the soul of a certain store manager one Christmas Eve as he stares out his window at the falling snow and, without even quite realizing what he is doing, weighs the meaning and fate of an abandoned baby?

"The Changeling," unlike "Mamba," is not a "true" story but rather is wholly a product of the author's imagination. At least, not quite wholly, for every such work contains at least a grain or two of fact. In this case I had been leafing through a medical journal when I came across a startling pair of "before" and "after" photographs depicting the results of plastic surgery upon a man whose face had been half eaten away by a long-lingering carcinoma of the nose. The caption under the "before" picture recounted with chilling brevity something of the man's history, telling how for years he had lived all alone and friend-less, eking out a welfare existence in some drab rooming house. In fact (and this was the detail that most riveted my attention), so agonizingly self-conscious had the fellow been about his ugly disfigurement that he had not dared set foot outside his one dingy room during daylight hours, but instead made a practice of venturing forth only late at night, and then just to the corner store to buy the few groceries he needed. And this was a situation that had persisted for some eighteen years!

I tried to think my way into the horror of such a life, but I could not. At least I doubted whether I could write honestly about it. And though naturally I was glad for the medical miracle that had finally rescued the sufferer and restored him to a more normal life, at the same time I found my thoughts about him wandering down a different path. I began to muse upon how God might have worked in such a life, if somehow a man like this had been granted the grace to believe in Jesus.

And that is where Joe Szloboda made his entrance. I envisioned a character with the sort of defect that would have crippled him not only visibly but invisibly, destroying his life both inside and out. And then I saw the Lord reaching out and touching that place of desolation, and not simply healing it but in the process making the defect itself the very means for drawing the wounded person into a deep love affair with Himself. "Blessed are those whose strength is in You," sings the Psalmist. "As they pass through the Valley of Tears, it becomes a place of springs!" (Ps. 84:6). Finally I tried to imagine the effects that such a transformation might have upon a world itself suffering and doomed (if not by obvious infirmity, then by its very appearance of "health") and so locked away in its own dingy room of horror.

Thus was born "The Changeling," a story that deals at different levels with the unsettling issue of the "miraculous," or of divine intervention—with the mystery of how it is that a supernatural God goes about meddling in the natural lives of His creatures, and the possible results of such intervention both for those who believe and for those who do not.

The story itself states plainly its central mystery: what exactly is the miracle here? Or can it be said that anything truly out of the ordinary takes place at all? Let us grant, for instance, that the little baby found in the department store creche had not simply materialized there, but was in all likelihood nothing more exotic than what the obtusely frank store manager surmised it to be—an infant abandoned by a prostitute. Nevertheless, is it not the case that some sort of true Incarnation does take place in this story? Is there not some fleshing out of mystery, some definite incursion of divinity into the realm of the mundane? And if so, how does it happen exactly? What is the miracle here?

Well, a man loses his stutter, yes. That is one thing. "The tongue of the stammerer becomes fluent and clear" (Isa. 32:4), just the sort of event the prophets said would take place in the Kingdom of God. I have occasionally heard about and have also met people whom Christ has miraculously delivered from a lifelong problem with stuttering. It is a small enough thing for God to do. Yet still there are always those who would explain such things away as being psychological phenomena or the like. For real miracles, if they *are* real, raise all kinds of awkward and infuriating questions, such as: if God really heals, why doesn't He do so for everyone, as a matter of course? Or why does He allow disease in the first place? Oddly enough the main effect of a miracle of healing upon the outside world can be to compound disbelief.

Yet behind every physical miracle lies another kind of supernatural event, a miracle of grace, without which the physical sign may be rendered worthless or even invisible. In "The Changeling" the first scene is that of a grown man opening his mouth to the sky and receiving a Communion wafer of snow upon his tongue. And throughout the story such moments of grace continue to drift down out of heaven like big snowflakes, accumulating on fenceposts and on people, and even on "one black cat huddled among the garbage cans." Does this latter image, perhaps, carry within it a faint suggestion of the scowling, doubting Mr. Thomas? And is it possible that the story's profoundest miracle occurs at the point where this man, in a moment pregnant with strange nostalgia, is caught with his head nodding before a window full of falling snow, as though the sky itself were floating down into his soul? However fleeting may be his subsequent vision of the Holy Child in the arms of an ungainly janitorial Madonna, still the reader senses that here something holy has happened, here some mystic seed has verily been planted in a stony heart, a seed that just might bear fruit, somewhere down the road, in a quietly amazing way.

Or is it more likely that just the opposite is true and that here Frank Thomas turns his back once and for all on the living Christ?

In any event, whether the store manager knows it or not, the reader certainly knows that here is a man who has been touched this Christmas Eve by the love of God—and make no mistake about it! And the story of the miraculous healing of an infirmity (whether that infirmity be a stutter or a deformed face and whether the agent of healing be a surgeon's knife or the hand of God) becomes secondary, almost incidental to the other and more subtle story lying behind this one, which is the story that tells (to quote from the popular carol "O Little Town of Bethlehem") "how silently, how silently, the wondrous gift is given."

For is not the greatest of all miracles, finally, the gospel itself? Here is the wonder to end all wonders, the supernatural act that heals the whole man all at once, through faith in a resurrected Savior. Surely this is a profound mystery. But it is also more than a mystery—more definable and tangible than any mere mystery—since the story of the gospel concerns not just a miraculous birth but a very unmiraculous death. In truth the story of Jesus as related in the four gospels is a type of murder mystery, and precisely for that reason it is not without its cold, hard facts, and neither is it without its inevitable and ingenious mousetrap of a solution.

A Scrap of Red

The Kumgang San, the fabled Diamond Mountains of North Korea, are so beautiful that it used to be said, before the division of the country into North and South, that every Korean wished to visit them before he died. At Pyongyang, the northern capital, in the year 1952, only two buildings were left standing in the entire city. Yet just over a hundred miles away the Diamond Mountains still stood, solid and dreaming, and their rivers still ran, east and south, as peacefully as ever across the war-torn border and on through Seoul and into the Yellow Sea. Throughout the war in the Kumgang San the lakes remained clear as a child's eyes, and from the forest-covered ridges the waterfalls continued to pour thick as sinews and white as forks of lightning, and there every pine tree still pointed straight up to its own personal star in the night sky.

In 1952 in a mud-walled farmhouse within sight of Kumgang, the highest of the peaks, a teenaged girl sat by the tiny window looking out over the valley and waited for the night. She watched as a huge sun dipped behind the brow of the mountains, suffusing the sky with gold. She was kneeling, and she was waiting for the twilight, for the darkness. It was a Sunday evening and Choi Sung Nam was waiting for the night so that she could go to church.

Along the pathway in front of her house workers were coming in from the fields. Although the sky was pouring its shining gold all over them, their forms looked shadowy, opaque, as if resistant to the light. This very moment, thought Choi Sung Nam, if only they could see it, all of them were walking along the very rim between light and darkness.

"Oh God," she prayed, with a nearly speechless longing. "Oh God."

Beyond the shadow figures, across the river, stood the silent line of mountains, drinking thirstily the sun's last rays. All along the highest ridges individual trees blazed like torches, and like golden mirrors on the lower slopes the terraced paddies gleamed. The harvest was just nearing its end and gold was everywhere.

When the number of passers-by had dwindled and the faces of the few figures left appeared dark as the mouths of caves, then Choi Sung Nam set out. Even if someone were to recognize her now, still there were many places she might be going. But she carried her little New Testament beneath her blouse, next to her skin, and she headed down to the river.

Finding the path along the bank, Choi Sung Nam proceeded out of the village toward the forest. Softly she hummed to herself, and in the deepening shadows the only other sound was the murmurous sliding of the water alongside her.

After a good walk she left behind the open fields and came to the edge of the trees and soon spotted firelight ahead. Emerging into the small clearing, she was surprised to see just two others there, seated on stumps close to the fire. They were Park, the one who led the services, and Kim, and as Choi Sung Nam arrived the men each rose to embrace her. And after that, although the three of them waited patiently, only one other man, Lee, showed up.

A month before there had been a congregation of ten. But one night the little abandoned building where they met had been burned. And in the following week two groups of Christians down the valley, fifteen persons in all, had been discovered at their worship and slaughtered on the spot.

For two weeks Choi Sung Nam and her friends had been too frightened even to contact one another. But now they were meeting once again, here in the woods, and there were four of them. It was November and the night was chilly, and the believers sat on stumps close to the fire, rubbing their hands together and discussing the recent events.

"Shrimp among whales," muttered Lee, citing an old Korean proverb. The words described the country's precarious position, surrounded on three sides by the mighty powers of China, the Soviet Union, and Japan. But now the proverb seemed much truer of the situation of Christians among the North Korean Communists.

Eventually Park opened their little service with the reading of some psalms. There would be no singing tonight, as there was too much danger of the sound carrying. So in voices that were near-whispers they read together, each one seeking to listen to the Word of God while at the same time keeping one ear attuned to the woods around.

"The angel of the Lord encamps around those who fear Him," they read. *"And He delivers them."*

The flames of the fire sucked and crackled. The wind stirred in the very tops of the pine trees. Farther off the river pumped like the moving of blood behind the ears. And a million other phantom sounds crowded the night.

"Be still," read the worshipers, *"and know that I am God."*

There followed a time of prayer. And very deep were the pleadings of the four united hearts: for peace; for their own safety; for comfort for the families of those who had been martyred; for the salvation of their enemies. Unlike the others, Choi Sung Nam kept her eyes wide open and gazed into the fire as she prayed.

Later Park stood up to speak. Tilting the pages of his Bible forward so that they caught the firelight, red-gold, he had to bow his head in order to read the tiny print. He was middle-aged, with a round face and small wire-framed glasses. Normally a flamboyant man, he would offer no theatrics tonight, no raising of the voice. The setting itself lent intensity to his message.

"Blessed are those who are persecuted because of righteousness, for theirs is the kingdom of heaven."

He read a verse or two, commented, then read some more, choosing passages from different places in the Scriptures. His voice, heartfelt, like a flame both burned and quavered.

Yet barely had he begun, and barely had the words of his texts begun to open like scented flowers into the night, when suddenly, almost as if the words themselves summoned out of the silent trees the very reality they signified, a dozen shadows emerged from the woods and stood in a circle all around the clearing. And each shadow cradled an automatic rifle.

Choi Sung Nam screamed but immediately clapped her own hand over her mouth to stifle the cry.

Park stopped in mid-sentence. Kim and Lee jumped to their feet and then shrank down again.

And now the very thing they all had most feared began to unfold before their eyes. One of the shadows stepped forward until his face came into the light: tallowy, pock-marked, flat-nosed, hard-eyed. This one carried his weapon slung over his shoulder, and his only uniform was a scrap of red cloth tied around one arm. Walking straight up to Park, he lifted the Bible out of Park's hands and held it aloft, still open, in the flat of one palm, like a platter.

"So tell me, great teacher," he began, in a tone of affected courtesy, "what fairy stories you are reading?"

Park remained silent. The fire spluttered.

"Come now," urged the guerilla soldier. "I know you can speak. I have just heard you. You speak very well. But will you not share your message with the rest of us? It must be a very wonderful message for you to gather out in the forest like this on a cold night. So tell us, please, what is this wonderful book of yours?"

Finding his voice with difficulty, Park replied, "It is God's book."

"God?" shot back the soldier. "God who? Who is this God?"

"He is our Father, the Creator of the whole world . . ."

"Stop!" The guerilla took a step closer. "Is this what is in your book?"

"Yes."

"And how deeply do you believe it?"

"With my whole heart," said Park simply.

"With your heart?"

"Yes."

"So," said the soldier, handing Park's Bible back to him and standing now with arms akimbo. "Prove to me."

Hesitantly Park began to leaf through his book.

"No!" barked the soldier. "No words! Action! I want action. I would *see* this heart of yours. Show me this heart that believes."

Park shrugged. He had no answer.

"I do not know what you mean," he stammered.

The soldier's reply was to stab his index finger into the center of Park's breast.

"Perhaps it would be easier to see this heart of yours," he said, "if we put a little hole in this chest." He cocked his head quizzically.

Park stared at the ground and answered, "I do not really think that would prove anything."

"You are right," said the guerilla. "So, so. But if we do not make a hole, then we must think of some other way for you to show us your heart."

Here he turned his back, paused significantly, and then said in a loud voice, as if addressing the trees, "Throw your Bible into the fire!"

Park took a deep breath. The whole forest whirled about him.

"Come!" shouted the guerilla. "Throw your wonderful book into the fire. Then we shall all see how deeply you believe."

Park spoke quietly. "This is the Word of God. I cannot throw it into the fire."

All at once, spinning around, the soldier yanked Park's glasses from his face and ground them into the dirt with his boot heel.

"Let us stop with the games," he said. "If you do not burn this Bible of yours and renounce your ridiculous religion, then we will fill you with holes. It is as simple as that. I will give the word, and you will be killed. You see? I am merciful. I am giving you a chance. All you have to do is to toss a little book into the fire. What could be simpler? Now—you have one second to decide."

For much longer than a second no one moved, no one spoke. The silent circle of leveled rifles seemed to constrict like a noose. The silver barrels were just visible in the shadows. They might have been the branches of trees glistening with lines of rainwater.

Park's hands froze around his Bible like clamps.

"I see you have trouble making up your mind," said the soldier finally. "But come, how about your friends here? Do they also have hearts that believe?"

Then, pointing at the man Kim, the commander motioned to one of the other guerillas, who stepped out of the shadows and placed the barrel of his weapon against Kim's chest.

"So, teacher," said the commander. "What do you say now? Is a book really worth more to you than the life of a friend? Come. All you need to do is to toss it into the fire. Set a good example for your disciples. Show them how deeply you believe."

Park wavered now. Burn a book, save a life. Was it not a simple computation?

From his seat on the stump Lee had dropped to his knees. Kim, for his part, was too frightened to move a muscle. He was a short, chubby man about the same age as Park. The barrel of the rifle was barely touching his coat, but it felt to him like the stab of a bayonet, or like a branding iron.

"In one second," said the commander, peering steadily at Park, "I am going to raise my arm. And when it comes down the believing heart of your friend will be blown out of his body. Then we can all have a good look at it."

Park seemed paralyzed now by indecision. His hands alternately tightened and loosened around the Bible, as though kneading it like dough.

Choi Sung Nam was staring into the fire and praying as hard as she knew how.

The commander raised his arm.

"Wait!" shouted Kim. It was a bloodcurdling wail, like the anguished cry of an animal. "I'll do anything you want! Please, please, please . . ." he whimpered.

For a few breathless moments the commander stood poised. Then, stepping toward Kim with his hand still upraised, he seized him by the scalp and lifted him trembling to his feet.

"So," he said. "So, so. The disciple is more reasonable than the teacher. Good. Good. Then tell me something, disciple. Tell me that you spit on God."

Kim stared, wide-eyed. His whole body shrank from where the tip of the rifle touched him .

"Say you spit on God! Say it!"

Against the small hard circlet of metal his heart pounded.

"I spit on God!" cried Kim, almost spitting the words out.

Dear Lord, prayed Choi Sung Nam, *forgive him. He does not know what he is saying.*

"Say you spit on Jesus Christ!" commanded the guerilla.

"I spit on Jesus Christ!" spat Kim.

God, be merciful. Forgive us all.

"Good, good," said the soldier. "You are doing well. Now put that book of yours where it belongs. Show your teacher how nicely it burns."

Without thought now, reacting with raw instinct, Kim flung his Bible immediately into the middle of the fire. For a moment, as though immune from all harm, the book lay perfectly still and intact within the purity of the flames. But then, slowly, it began to move, almost to breathe, puffing itself up and opening until each page stood out limned with a filigree of fire, and finally, with a withering implosion, the book caved into flames.

"Good boy! Good boy!" cheered the commander. "You should have a reward for that." And at a slight signal one of the guerillas stepped forward and rammed the butt of his rifle into Kim's plump stomach, leaving him doubled over and groaning.

"So," said the commander, ignoring Park and turning now toward Lee. "So. What about you? How much do you love your book? Will you also show us your heart?"

Lee was a lad of twenty, delicate-featured, a student. A lover of all books. But now the stiff finger of the rifle was against his chest, pointing, pressing. The finger of death.

Carefully Lee stood up. Even more carefully, making certain his every action was crystal clear, he took one step, bent down, and gently, almost reverently, placed his Bible at the edge of the fire. It was as though he meant to indicate by this smallest of gestures that he indeed still loved this book, even while consigning it to the flames.

Yet before he could rise to his feet, the commander had crept up behind him, and putting his boot against Lee's backside, he shoved hard so that the boy's whole body went sprawling right on top of the fire. Showers of sparks and coals spewed everywhere as Lee bounced straight up in the middle of the blaze and looked, for a moment, simply surprised, like a man dunked in cold water. Then he began yowling like a cat and rolling around in the dirt while all the guerilla soldiers clapped and hooted and guffawed.

God, God, help us, help us, prayed Choi Sung Nam. How dreadful it was for screams and laughter to be mixed.

But already the commander was back in front of Park and fixing him with a gaze that was an outrageous blend of amusement, pitilessness, and a strange intimacy.

"So, teacher. It is your turn again. You see how easy it is? A little book burns much easier than a man. Wouldn't you say so?"

And now the snout of the rifle was against Park's own chest. Smelling, nuzzling, as if scenting the blood inside.

No time now to think clearly of what was true and what was not. No time to think at all. Time only for whatever was inside of a man to come out, spontaneously, the pit of the heart indeed revealed in a single burst of light.

The commander raised his arm.

The forest whirled, then stood perfectly still.

And suddenly, trembling all over, Park shook his Bible out of his hand and into the fire. As if it were an insect that had been stinging him.

Immediately the soldier grabbed him by the hair.

"Say you curse God!" he growled.

Park shook his head.

"Say it!"

His lips trembled. The bore of the rifle jabbed hard between his ribs.

"Out with it!"

"I curse God," whispered Park.

"You spit on Jesus Christ!"

"I spit on Jesus Christ," whispered Park.

"Louder!"

"I spit on Jesus Christ," he said, louder.

"Shout it to the stars!"

"I spit on Jesus Christ!" he wailed into the top of the black and empty sky, into the endless cave of the universe. Park was a machine now, doing what he was told.

"There," said the soldier quietly, releasing his hold. "Doesn't it feel good?"

And then there came the roaring thud of the rifle butt into Park's gut.

My God, my God, why hast Thou . . .

If only I can keep on praying, thought Choi Sung Nam. If only I can say His name. If only I can cling to His cross.

For now it was her turn. Still seated on her stump, she kept her hands folded over the little New Testament in her lap. And as the guerilla commander stood over her and took her by the hair and tilted her eyes up to meet his, she looked into the very back of those eyes and thought one single word, "Jesus, Jesus, Jesus, Jesus, Jesus . . ."

The soldier pulled her to her feet.

"So, sister," he said softly. "Will you make it unanimous? Will you be a good girl and throw your Bible into the fire?"

"No," said Choi Sung Nam.

Flashing through her mind then came the memory of the curious manner in which she had acquired this New Testament. On a winter day beside the river, she had spotted a patch of something bright red caught high in a tree branch. Fishing it down, she found the little book attached to a piece of shriveled rubber. Later she had learned about a group of Christians in the south who, whenever winds blew northwards, would range along the hilltops and release balloons freighted with Bibles toward their Communist brothers.

"Come!" urged the guerilla soldier. "Show us your heart. Throw your book into the fire."

Choi Sung Nam was seventeen, younger even than Lee. But her mind was made up.

"No," she repeated. Plainly, without blinking. "I will not deny the truth."

And then the tiny metal mouth of the rifle came against her left breast, probing obscenely, and she felt it there blunt as a kiss, sharp as the bite of a nail.

"Now," said the commander. "Tell me again about truth."

"The truth is not in your guns," said Choi Sung Nam simply. "The truth is in the Lord Jesus Christ."

Her boldness amazed her. Was there something about being a woman, she wondered, that made this gun a less fearful thing than it had been for the men?

But now the soldier was putting his face directly in front of hers, as if he were about to kiss her, and when he spoke she could feel his lips brushing against hers.

He was saying filthy things. Making threats. Tugging harder on her scalp.

But she thought only, "Jesus, Jesus, Jesus . . ."

And finally she spoke it out loud, into the midst of his filth. "Don't you realize? Jesus loves you! Jesus loves you!"

And at that, recoiling, he slapped her hard with the back of his hand.

"Sister," he sneered, "this is no game."

"You are very right," said Choi Sung Nam.

There was the slightest, the most mysterious pause, the smallest hint of a stand-off, during which Choi Sung Nam took courage and went on. "If you kill me, I know I will go to heaven. But what about you? I am ready to lose my life in this world. Are you ready to lose yours in eternity?"

At that the commander drew back and raised his arm. "Throw that Bible into the fire," he barked, "or in one second you will be shot!"

Seconds went by. Choi Sung Nam closed her eyes. The metal dug towards her heart. Out loud she prayed, "Father, forgive them . . ."

And then the arm came down.

And in the center of her chest, and all through her body, Choi Sung Nam felt a dry, cold, hollow, *click*. Like the slightest knock against the door of her heart. It was the sound of the rifle's trigger.

But when she opened her eyes there was still, amazingly, the fire in front of her, and still the commander of the guerilla soldiers standing right there, and behind him Park, Kim, and Lee, all on the ground, and still she clutched her New Testament, and still the metal smelled her breast, and still there was the ring of rifles all around, and the dark pine trees, and still the wind in their very tops, and still the distant solemn sliding of the river through the night like blood beneath the earth. And still, and forever, printed upon Choi Sung Nam's heart was the memory of the small, cold, empty *knock*.

Then once again, bringing his face in close to hers, though not so indecently close as before, the commander was speaking to her. Yet this time, spread across the sallow face and garishly lighting every corner of it, was a broad and enigmatically triumphant smile.

"Sister," he was saying. "You are the winner! You are the winner!" And then in a whisper, "That rifle was never loaded."

And turning to the rest of his men he called out, "Take those other three cowards and shoot them. But this girl—let her go free. She is the one with the heart. She is the true Christian."

Fiction's Surprise

The last shall be first, and the first last.

—MATTHEW 20:16

The surprise ending is a narrative device as old as stories themselves and one that Jesus employed regularly in His parables. The parable of the workers in the vineyard in Matthew 20 is a classic example: industrious day-laborers, after slaving for twelve hours in the hot sun, are crestfallen when told that the wage they have earned will be exactly the same as that of some shiftless no-goods who have worked alongside them for just one hour. Not only are we surprised in this parable at the idea that equal pay should be offered for unequal work but Jesus gives the story a final twist with the paradoxical moral that the first shall be last.

Similarly, when the Master concludes the parable of the rich fool in Luke 12 with the unforgettable line, "This very night your life will be required of you," He is introducing this same element of sudden and unforeseen indignity, a wrenching turning-of-the-tables that, by casting all preceding events in a new light, forces a radical reinterpretation of the entire story.

Of course the device of surprise need not be reserved for the very end of a story in order to be effective. Matthew's grisly version of the parable of the wedding banquet, to cite just one example, depends throughout upon a continuous barrage of the absurd and the unexpected. The story opens tamely enough, depicting a king preparing a sumptuous feast for the celebration of his son's marriage and sending out his servants to extend invitations. But very soon things take a weird turn, when for reasons that are entirely obscure the invited guests refuse to come. And not only that, but when the invitations are graciously reissued, suddenly the behavior of the guests turns bizarrely and disproportionately savage. They seize, abuse, and murder the king's servants, whereupon the king is driven to retaliate by sending in his army to destroy the whole city. Finally, as the banquet gets underway with a brand new roster of guests, one of these is all at once accosted by the host, bound hand and foot, and brutally expelled, having apparently committed no other offense than that of being inappropriately dressed for the feast.

What is going on here? Why all this fuss over an ordinary wedding banquet? Doesn't everybody love a big feed? The ending comes as a shocker, but really no more so than many of the events preceding it. The entire effect of the story rests upon the maintenance of a nail-biting atmosphere in which anything at all might happen at any moment and in which surprise becomes the rule rather than the exception.

What does this element of surprise—together with a host of related ingredients such as crisis, suspense, shock, violence, and absurdity—accomplish in fiction? Probably much the same thing as such elements accomplish in real life: they pull out rugs, rip off masks, and crack people wide open. They are devices calculated, in other words, to throw characters off balance, and to do so in such a way that whatever is truly inside of them can come spilling out. For it is in awkward, unguarded moments that the most intimate interior secrets of personalities can be exposed. And that, after all, is the central concern of fiction, as it is of life—the revelation, the laying bare, of the deepest motives of the human heart. Literature is a kind of laboratory of human nature, an operating theatre in which the soul is laid out on a white table and sliced open, at any cost, to see what is in there. And surprise is one of the scalpels, an instrument with an edge so keen as to be, at its best, invisible. If you can see a surprise coming, it isn't the real thing.

"A Scrap of Red," being a war story, contains a good deal of exploratory surgery. For that is what war is like, and literature has always exploited the tense, freakish, white-knuckled explosiveness of the war environment as an experimental means of exerting the ultimate pressure upon its characters (just the way it also exploits the wild, unpredictable territory of romantic love). Like the parable of the wedding banquet, this story depends for its effect upon an atmosphere in which all the normal checks and balances of daily life have been suspended and replaced by a climate of scandalous uncertainties. Yet in this case even this is but preparatory groundwork leading up to the culminating shocker, a conclusion so outrageous and improbable that it turns the rest of the story inside out. The surprise ending is the thing that makes this story "work," the very thing for which the rest of the story was written. For somehow in the guerilla commander's final, swift, irrational judgment, truth spills its guts, and there is a sense in which some sort of ultimate justice, perversely but thrillingly, is satisfied.

Thomas Merton's last public lecture, entitled "Marxism and Monastic Perspectives" and delivered just hours before his sudden death in Bangkok, contains an anecdote about a conference he had attended in California, to which many student revolutionary leaders had been invited. In a lull between lectures Merton had introduced himself to a group of these students as a Trappist monk, whereupon one of the young Marxists immediately responded, "We also are monks."

In "A Scrap of Red," is there something of this same line of reasoning lying behind the Communist guerilla leader's capricious decision to spare the life of Choi Sung Nam? Does he see in her heart, perhaps, the same telltale marking that he wears on his own sleeve—a scrap of red? Does he sense, in other words, that the courage of conviction required of a true Christian is the same sort of courage demanded of a guerilla soldier fighting in a bloody civil war? Or are there other motives causing him to behave as he does?

Whatever his reasons, the fact is that the central concern of the story is this subtle matter of *motive*. What makes the man act this way? What does his behavior accomplish for him? How ironic it is that an atheistic soldier should unwittingly enact the just judgment of God upon a group of Christians! Or does he? And what about the motives of the other characters? Why, exactly, does Choi Sung Nam find the courage to put her life on the line, while the three other Christians do not? And to what extent (and in whose eyes?) does the weakness of the others constitute a real apostasy?

The ramifications are many, but all such questions boil down to one: What *drives* these characters at the core of their beings? What makes each one of them *tick*? All the narrative trappings of surprise and suspense and violence are aimed at disclosing this central secret, the well-kept secret of motivation. For the human heart, largely obscure even to itself, is no easy safe to crack. Dynamite is called for, and even then it must be said that people's deepest motives, emerging out of layer upon layer of darkly subtle influences, are essentially fathomless, known finally to God alone.

But right here is the fundamental territory explored by all fiction—the terra incognita of the human heart, with its tangled and hidden drives. And nowhere in the world's literature is this heart of darkness more deeply probed than it is in the simple parables of Jesus. Moreover in the case of the Lord's stories it is not just the human heart that is revealed, but also the heart of God. This was Jesus' own motive in telling stories (for God has motives too)—to reveal the loving heart of the Father and at the same time to expose the sinfulness at the bottom of, at the driving center of, the heart of man.

Would it be overly naive to propose that this same double-pronged thrust should be the goal of all serious literature and particularly of that written by Christians? And would it be equally naive to suggest that *surprise*—the sudden and preposterously neat turning of the world on its ear—might be the principal method available to storytelling for the accomplishment of this most difficult operation of bringing people face to face with their God? A parable, after all, has something in common with a good joke, in that much of its impact hinges upon eliciting an immediate and spontaneous response. For the jester the goal is laughter, but for the Christian storyteller surely the desired response has to do with the conviction of the Holy Spirit. Yet if a joke or a parable has to be explained, all of its effect is lost. There can be a kind of intellectual grasp of the point of a story, but only an authentic, cleansing *surprise*—the laughter of the soul—can spark true illumination.

In the final analysis the thing that is perhaps most surprising of all about "A Scrap of Red" may not be its ending per se but just the sobering fact that, like "Mamba," this story is essentially a true one. While I have not seen the original account, I've been told it appeared some years ago in a missionary magazine, and although once again I have taken certain artistic liberties in "fictionalizing" it, the changes I have made are not such as to distort or exaggerate the underlying facts. It is a simple matter of truth that somewhere in Korea, not so long ago, the Lord Himself sifted hearts among a little group gathered around a campfire, and the results—as is always the case with God—were most surprising. For surprise is one of the Lord's hallmarks. True, overwhelming, purgative surprise is one of the ways we can know that it is the living God we have to deal with, not some impostor.

In fact, is there not something in this phenomenon of the "final twist," the swift upending of all expectations and the last-minute total reversal of fortunes, that encapsulates the very essence of the gospel itself? In all Jesus' teaching and storytelling what happens so often is that the ordinary surface of the world is rent (as the veil of the temple was torn at the Crucifixion), and in that tear the truth is revealed. For in the Kingdom of God the world's applecart is upset, so that the humble are exalted, the blind see, the weak become strong, poverty turns to riches, and in the last dark moments victory is irrevocably snatched from the jaws of defeat.

"For suddenly, in an instant, the Lord Almighty will come!" (Isa. 29:5).

The Ghost of Christmas

A. B. was what his daughter Rita liked to call a "buttonholer." He fastened onto people and wouldn't let go until he had told them more than they ever wanted to know about Jesus. He was not above pointing his long, bony index finger like the barrel of a loaded gun directly at the center of a man's chest, while resting the other hand companionably on the fellow's shoulder, ready to clamp down like a vise should he try to wriggle away. That, at least, was how Rita saw it.

Rita was certainly right that, whether you were a dinner guest in her father's home or a stranger waiting at a bus stop, A. B. had but one thing on his mind: to tell you how to get saved (or, if you were saved already, how to find the Lord's will). Even his closest friends liked to joke that "A. B. loved you and had a wonderful plan for your life." After all, what else was there to talk about besides God? Who had time to chatter away about politics and baseball or to be suave and urbane, as if pleasantness alone could ensure one a place in heaven? Was not life like a puff of smoke, like a flower of the field that bloomed one day and withered the next? The cashier who rang up your groceries on Friday afternoon, smiling and perky, might be dead Friday night, without ever having known the love of Jesus. So the human predicament was desperate, catastrophic. Every moment eternity hung in the balance; staggering issues clamored for attention. And if most people insisted upon spending their lives frantically avoiding those very issues, what better service could A. B. perform than to insist upon bringing the issues patiently but pressingly back to their attention? If A. B. had a childlike faith, he also had a child's capacity to aggravate.

For always at the back of his mind was God's warning to Ezekiel: "If you do not speak out to dissuade the wicked man from his ways, that wicked man will die in his sin, and I will hold you accountable for his blood." A. B. sincerely did not want to be responsible for any man not knowing the way of salvation. Yet at the same time this was far more than a matter of religious duty with him. The fact was that after decades of missionary work in Korea the gospel simply welled up out of his heart irrepressibly. He talked automatically of the Lord, the way others talked of the weather, and as others quoted the *Reader's Digest* or whatever they had heard on the news that day, so A. B. quoted from God's Word. He seemed to breathe the Scriptures. "A beautiful day, A. B.!" someone might greet him. "Yes!" he would reply heartily. "The Sun of Righteousness has risen with healing in His wings!" And then he would be off and running.

A. B. had had some astounding successes. One of his favorite stories was that of the vacuum cleaner salesman who had knocked on his door one day many years before and had ended up staying for a month while A. B. discipled him. Now the man was pastor of a large church in California. Another time a young customs official had made the mistake of asking A. B. if he was carrying any liquor in the car. That fellow ended up working with Wycliffe Bible Translators in New Guinea. And there were dozens of such tales. In fact, if one could possibly have totaled up the number of people A. B. had led to the Lord, taking into account too that new converts would in turn carry the message to others in an ever-widening network— well, it was simply staggering the impact that one man could have in advancing the Kingdom of God.

A. B. took great comfort in this thought. But he also knew he was only a farmer, scattering seed. Much of the seed was bound to fall by the wayside, on rocks or into thorns, and be wasted. But some of it, he knew, would fall on good soil, and produce a crop of fifty or a hundredfold. And that was the seed that counted. It was his job to broadcast the seed; it was the Lord's job to make it grow.

Perhaps A. B. even looked a little like a farmer. His face and neck and hands (and those parts alone) were brown as dirt from a life spent largely outdoors. He was tall and skinny as a post, and about as wooden in the way he walked, and when he stood still he seemed to lean somewhat, as if facing into a strong wind. His Adam's apple jutted out like a bone swallowed the wrong way. And in his eyes there was the look of someone who searches the skies, who is accustomed to peering off into the farthest distances, checking the horizon. There was the look, if it is possible, of great long-suffering combined with eager anticipation.

Of late, however, A. B.'s confidence had been failing him. Instead of giving thanks for all that the Lord had done through him in his long life, he had given way to an unaccustomed discouragement, or more precisely, a disgruntlement, over what the Lord was not doing. He found himself bothered more and more by the barren soil. Was there really nothing to be done about it? And had he himself, perhaps, contributed to its barrenness? In particular his thoughts focused upon his daughter Rita. His five other children were born-again Christians, serving the Lord in various parts of the world. His two oldest sons had actually followed him to Korea and were this moment working on additions to the school and hospital complex he had built, as well as preaching in the open air and leading Bible studies just as he had done for forty years. One other son was a missionary doctor in Africa, ministering not far from where the heart of David Livingstone was buried. As for A. B.'s two youngest daughters, they were not, he had to admit, leading lives that were quite so dramatically evangelistic. They had settled down with good but unambitious husbands and were raising families. They had their color television sets and their microwave ovens and A. B. found them, quite frankly, rather dull to talk to. They had never caught the missionary visicn. But at least they knew the Lord, and that was the main thing.

With Rita, however, it was a different story. Rita was the sole holdout. While the other girls were quiet and obedient creatures, pretty and feminine, Rita was a large, big-boned woman, tough, raucously jovial, and stubborn as the day was long. Where had this one come from? A. B. often wondered. It was almost as if she were of a different cut entirely from the rest of the family (although perhaps the truth was that she was so much like her father that neither of them could really appreciate the resemblance). In any case she had a mind of her own and had always said exactly what she thought. If A. B. were an evangelist for the Lord, then Rita too practised her own brand of evangelism, and it was quite decidedly not a religious one.

Rita had made one big mistake in her life. At twenty-five, when she ought to have known better, she had let a man sleep with her. But worse than that, it was a man she had known only a few days and who had not even cared for her body, let alone for her, but only for a night of sex. Of course Rita had known this. She was not stupid. But she had quite simply been overcome by desire. Even as a teenager, before she put on weight, she had not had many dates. So it had been a moment of weakness, that was all, like reaching for a chocolate eclair. It could have happened to anyone.

But the result was a child.

A. B., who had not been back from Korea in five years, had seen Charlotte only as a baby. But when the Mission Board forced him to retire (that was a story in itself) and he returned home to settle down in the same city as Rita, it was at least partly with the idea of having some impact upon this grand-daughter of his (and perhaps even upon Rita herself) before it was too late. In fact, he had actually had a dream in which he felt the Lord promising him success if he went to live near his wayward daughter. Accordingly he purchased a small house in a neighboring suburb. It was a broken-down thing, held together mostly by years of grime, but A. B. was a frugal man who appreciated a bargain.

Rita had met him at the airport, and for the first few days things went extremely well. She had bent over backwards to help her father get settled in. Together they cleaned the whole filthy house in three days, from stem to stern, almost until it gleamed, working shoulder to shoulder and even joshing around like old army buddies. They both were garrulous and shared a robust and eccentric sense of humor. Charlotte, tiny as she was, joined eagerly in the work. She could scarcely carry a pail of water without spilling most of it, but she was a bright, well-behaved girl, and A. B. took an instant shine to her.

Having finished the inside of the house, the crew moved outside, and father and daughter shared secrets of carpentry. It was the height of summer, and as they scrubbed, nailed, scraped, and painted, towering white clouds scudded overhead like tall ships in the cerulean sky. Evenings were cool and luminous, and after their work the three of them would sit out in the backyard around a hibachi until the mosquitoes drove them inside. Then, with Charlotte asleep on the couch, Rita and A. B. would stay up talking and talking in the manner of family members who, separated for years and having little in common anymore, nevertheless shared in their mutual past a kind of lost innocence.

Strange as it might sound, there were even ways in which A. B. (although he himself would not have admitted to this) actually felt closer to Rita than to any of his other children. And yet in the final analysis, what real fellowship could believers have with unbelievers?

The trouble began, of course, when A. B. started his buttonholing. How would Charlotte like a color storybook about an exciting hero named Jesus? And wouldn't she enjoy coming to church with her old grandpa? Did she know there was such a thing as salvation?

Rita hit the roof. One of these conversations, right under her nose, she let pass. But the second time it happened she actually stood up from her lawn chair, a loaded hamburger dripping ketchup down her arm, and gave A. B. one of her notorious "teacher stares," grim enough to stop a locomotive. She taught junior high and brooked no nonsense from anyone, including the principal.

For a few tense moments nothing had been said. Mother boiled, the little girl crept to the edge of her chair, and Grandpa looked a portrait of innocence. Eventually, once Rita gained a semblance of control she said, "Dad, we're happy to have you here." She spoke in measured tones, as if counting out A. B.'s allowance. "But there will be no discussion of religion in this family. You know the problems it's always caused in the past. Charlotte wants a grandpa, not a propagandist."

Rita had learned well from her father; the only way to handle A. B. was to be more assertive, more intimidating, than he was.

And so a line had been drawn. At least Rita had drawn her line; it was not yet clear where A. B. would draw his. He decided to limit his evangelizing to private conversations with the girl, explaining carefully to her that it might be better if mother didn't know when they had talked of "certain matters." But of course mother did know; she grilled her daughter on every detail of her times alone with Grandpa. She loved the old man, in her strong-willed, big-hearted way, but when it came to this business of religion she trusted him no more than if he had been one of her junior-high boys. He had a one-track mind, and she was determined that Charlotte not be swallowed up in his fanaticism. Perhaps it was her one deepest fear that some day the girl might rebel and actually become a Christian. Charlotte was all she had. How could she stand to have her own daughter side against her, just as the rest of the family always had?

So very soon there came a second confrontation with A. B., in which she told him pointblank that if he ever again so much as breathed the name of Jesus around Charlotte, she would cut off their visits altogether. "I'm not fooling, Dad. I'm not having you pump my daughter full of religion." Rita had a way of planting her feet, arms akimbo, that made her look like the entire defensive line of a football team.

A. B., however, was not inexperienced as a quarterback. His whole life had been devoted to smuggling the gospel past all opposition, and there was something in this second warning of Rita's that served only to whet his zeal. He had always considered it a much healthier thing—at least here in North America—when people openly resisted the faith rather than pretended to be Christians when really they were not. Indeed the very extremity of Rita's reaction might even be a sign that she was closer than anyone could know to surrendering. Besides, had not the gospel always thrived under persecution? At least now the battle lines were clearly drawn, and A. B. warmed to the task ahead. Truly he was in his element. He prayed up a storm. His Adam's apple worked overtime. Putting himself entirely in the Lord's hands, and fully confident of the inherent power of the gospel, A. B. set about evangelizing his granddaughter more brazenly than ever.

The third confrontation was a calm one—a long, cool, rational talk. A meeting between generals. But it was A. B. who eventually gained the upper hand, pointing out to Rita how totally unreasonable were her demands. The gospel was the plain truth, he said, and could not be suppressed. Did she expect Charlotte to go through life without ever having to deal with the great questions of faith, without ever thinking it through for herself? Did she expect to keep her in the dark about Jesus Christ, the most famous man in history? Did she actually think she could protect her daughter from everything she herself did not agree with? Besides, he argued, his Christianity was so much a part of him that he could not possibly be silent about it. Take that away from him, and he was nobody. Did Rita want Charlotte to have a nobody for a grandfather? A fake, an impostor? Or would she be allowed, rather, to get to know her grandpa in 3-D and technicolor, as the full-blooded old rapscallion of a missionary that he was?

A. B. felt his case was so convincing, so watertight, that he began to believe he might be winning over his daughter. She listened to him so patiently, grew so very quiet, and in the end offered no more arguments of her own—except, as it turned out, the argument of total intransigence. For finally she looked him straight in the eye and said, "Dad, it's plain to me that when it comes to religion you are not a sane man. You are determined to infect Charlotte with your bigoted views, even against the wishes of her own mother. Therefore, since it is obvious you cannot control yourself, you leave me no choice but to forbid you to have anything more to do with her. From now on you are not to try to see Charlotte under any circumstances, and until you agree to change your mind on this issue and refrain from proselytizing, I'm afraid you are no longer welcome in our home. I'm sorry, but I cannot see any other solution. Perhaps you will come to your senses."

And that had been the end of that. Nothing could be more fierce than a cornered mother.

Initially A. B. had not really believed she could be in earnest. He had not seriously considered that it might come to this. Of course wherever the gospel was preached there was bound to be opposition. Deep and determined hostility was to be expected. Had not Jesus warned, "A man's enemies will be the members of his own household?" But the willful severing of blood ties—that was not a thing to be done lightly. Surely, given time, the thing would blow over.

But it did not blow over. Three times in the next two weeks A. B. phoned his daughter and remonstrated with her. But always her answer was the same: A. B. was the one who was making things difficult, not she. If he were a sex maniac, or insisted on giving Charlotte drugs, then her reaction would have been the same. She was simply setting clear limits, as any parent had to do these days. It was up to A. B. to respect those limits. Parents, and not grandparents, must have the final word in a child's upbringing.

One day A. B. showed up on Rita's doorstep and was actually turned away. By his own daughter! How many times had he changed her diapers? And now he found himself standing on her steps in a September drizzle, with the door shut in his face. He couldn't get over it. The thing just wouldn't sink in. Clearly, as unsavory as it might sound, his daughter must be in the grip of the Devil. Or could it be the Lord Himself who, for reasons known only to Him, had hardened her heart just as He had done with Pharaoh?

"Blessed are they which are persecuted for righteousness' sake," Jesus had promised, and of course on one level A. B. was thrilled and actually rejoiced that he was being scorned and rejected on account of the gospel. But beyond that (and was this at an even deeper level?) he was in agony. A month went by, then two. He threw himself into the work of the local church but could find no peace. The image of his little grand-daughter haunted him. He pleaded with the Lord to show him what to do, but no clear answer would come. Should he just give in? But that was unthinkable. To accede to Rita's demands would be to deny his Lord, his very soul. Had not Jesus said, "He who denies me before men, I will deny before my Father?" What then could he do? His hands were tied. It was utterly inconceivable for him to carry on a relationship without ever talking of Christ, without any bold witness to His love and glory. It would be like trying to avoid the word *and* or *the* in conversation or to get along without any vowels. What was left to say?

For Rita's part, teaching junior high had inured her to battles of the will. Could any human beings on earth be more headstrong than pubescent teenagers? But Rita prided herself upon being able to hold out against any of them. She planted her feet and refused to budge; it was as simple as that. And the same methods that worked in the classroom she applied to the larger arena of life, treating the world as a school, other adults as children, and children as human beings reduced to simplest terms. When it came to her father, therefore, it wasn't that Rita had actually disowned him; she had simply sent him out into the hall to cool his heels. When he was good and ready, when he was prepared to behave himself, he could come back. All her life Rita had resisted his religious nonsense, and she wasn't about to yield now. A. B. was a powerful, persuasive, stubborn man, one in whom there was no separating the single-mindedness from the narrow-minded-ness, the virtue from the fault. Rita knew that if she gave him so much as an inch, he would swallow her whole. Perhaps the very secret to her strength of character was this opposition to her father, this capacity for outmaneuvering him.

Both father and daughter, therefore, tended to view things in black-and-white terms. But while for Rita, in the present crisis, this made for simplicity, A. B. found himself squirming amidst a growing complexity. Was it simply that parents were always more deeply and maddeningly attached to their chil-dren than vice versa? In any case whatever suffering the rift may have caused for Rita was skillfully suppressed and repu-diated, as a soldier must repudiate the suffering of war, and she lost no sleep over the affair. And being unaware of the depth of her own pain, neither could she have any idea of what A. B. was going through. He was a tough old bird, wasn't he? A sort of veteran politician of religion?

But Charlotte had started first grade, and as the long, light-filled summer days shrank away into fall the old man torment-ed himself with the thought of all the precious moments he would be missing in the development of his granddaughter. She would actually be learning how to read. Soon she would be capable of studying God's Word for herself. But would the estrangement from her Christian grandfather turn her away from Christ forever? And what kind of lies would Rita be tell-ing the child about him? That he was nothing but a maniac, a religious nut, a dangerous old fool to be avoided like the plague? How impressionable was a young mind! And then there was the question of Rita herself. Where had A. B. gone wrong with her? All these years he had prayed unceasingly for her conversion, but of course being on the opposite side of the globe had made it much easier to leave her in the hands of the Lord. Now, in his retirement, he was being brought face to face all over again with his failure as a Christian father, with his failure to impress the love of Jesus upon one so near and dear to him.

Contrary to his nature A. B. actually began to give way to depression. He brooded, lost his appetite, grew listless. These things had never happened to him before. Never had he been so tested. He had faced difficult situations in the past, had often been under enormous stress. But he was an optimistic sort, not easily discouraged even for an hour. Why was he being affected so grievously now? Of course part of the problem was his forced retirement; no more carrying the gospel to the ends of the earth, no more living out there on the very cutting edge of the Kingdom from moment to moment. Now he was stuck in this backwater of a North American suburb, out in the boondocks of faith. His sons had even joked that he would be getting a color television and a microwave oven and taking up lawn bowling and cribbage. These thoughts rattled him, like mice running around a wire cage in his mind.

Still, it was no reason to give up hope, to stop trusting in the Lord. No reason was good enough for that. What business did a Christian have moping around? "Rejoice in the Lord," said the Apostle. "And again I say, Rejoice!" Yet more and more, as the months wore on, A. B. could find no joy, no peace. Though he searched the Scriptures for consolation and direction, somehow it was the passages of warning and censure that lodged in his mind. "If a man know not how to rule his own house," wrote Paul to Timothy, "how shall he take care of the church of God?" At such words A. B.'s whole ministry came before him in question. Had he preached the gospel to others, only to be disqualified himself? Could it be that all these years his witnessing had been without love and therefore worthless? Was he nothing but sounding brass, a tinkling cymbal? For the first time he could ever remember (actually it had happened before, but he had forgotten), A. B. experienced a prolonged inability to pray. Rather than pouring out all his concerns in a flood of words like a little child to his Father, as had always been his custom, he tended now to sit mute before the Lord, both his tongue and his heart frozen tight. Sometimes he felt nothing at all, other times he was a tangled mass of hurt and confusion, even moaning and groaning out loud like an animal. Occasionally in his frustration he even yelled at God, bawling Him out for not answering. What on earth was going on? Could it be that he was losing his mind? Or worse than that, his faith? A man who insisted on fretting, who would not let go of his problems and surrender them to the Lord, was a man who did not believe.

Another month went by, and another. Snow came, melted once, then came to stay. The daylight dwindled and the night sky grew black as an open grave above the white earth. The stars were brighter than they were in summer, but also farther away, and they shone with a cold light.

On one of these nights, just a week before Christmas, A. B. was poring over his Bible, following each line with his index finger as he always did. He was in the opening chapter of Luke, preparing for a study of that evangelist's incandescent account of the first Christmas. But first he came to the story of Zechariah, the father of John the Baptist, and all at once a peculiar feeling began to creep over him, almost a kind of spell. It was like the uncanny feeling one might occasionally experience when some ordinary sound (running water, for instance, or the flickering of a fire) seemed suddenly to be transformed into clear, audible music, as though a marching band were winding its way through distant streets or perhaps crowding right into one's living room. But the sound A. B. heard now, as he bent over his Bible that December evening, was not one of music but rather of the voice of the Lord God Himself speaking to him, and saying, "Behold, thou shalt be dumb, and not able to speak, because thou believest not my words, which shall be fulfilled in their season." They were the words of the twentieth verse, in which Zechariah, seeing a vision of the angel Gabriel and yet doubting the divine message, was struck dumb, unable to speak another word until the angel's promise had come true.

A. B. stared at the page, his mouth dry and hollow. He knew the story well, but this time as he read it something had moved inside him, shifted, like plates of the earth's crust or like a fetus moving in its mother's womb. There was a kick, a pang of queasy pain yet also of wonder, and then a slow subterranean explosion took place, as though some hard wad of congestion deep inside him were being dislodged, blown apart. "The word of God is quick and powerful," wrote the author of Hebrews, "and sharper than any two-edged sword, piercing even to the dividing asunder of soul and spirit, and of the joints and marrow."

And in that moment something new came flooding into A. B.'s heart, something new and great and inexpressibly wonderful.

The very next morning was the presentation of the annual children's Christmas pageant at A. B.'s church. This year it was a mime, and there was none of the excruciating woodenness of children reciting lines. Not a word was spoken. There was only the dreamlike solemnity of small bodies draped in bath towels shuffling back and forth across the stage. The congregation craned their necks to see, chuckled, exchanged wry and puzzled glances. But A. B. covered his face and wept. The message was all too clear; for whatever reasons the privilege of speech had been taken away from him. The thing he had most depended upon all his life could no longer be used. He was like a boxer with both hands tied behind his back. Like Zechariah, he had the most wonderful news to share with the world and especially with Rita and Charlotte. But he could not open his mouth. Nevertheless, perhaps the Lord could still make use of him, just as he had used Zechariah, working through a man's silence even more powerfully than through his speech.

For the next few days A. B. was like a patient emerging from a long illness. The daylight hurt his eyes. The world seemed such a vast and bewildering place. His legs felt like rubber. He had planned to visit two dozen hospital patients in

the week before Christmas, but he didn't have the energy. His
stomach was unsettled and he ate little. He felt strangely ten-
der, inside and out, and often on the verge of tears. All he
wanted to do was to sit still in a chair and be with God. He
seemed lost in some glory, immobilized by wonder. For when
the root of despair has finally been exposed, then it begins to
shrivel, and perhaps it is the wizened detritus of despair that
goes to make up joy.

Two days before Christmas A. B. phoned Rita and told her
he was ready to give in. He had been wrong, he admitted,
stubborn as an old mule. Would she forgive him? And
couldn't they spend Christmas together? He would promise to
respect her wishes and say nothing to Charlotte about religion. They would just have a nice day, play some games and
eat some turkey, make up for the months of hurt.

If Rita had believed in the Lord, she might have fallen on
her knees at that moment and thanked Him for this miracle.
As it was, she was inclined to be skeptical. The granting of
forgiveness could be harder even than the asking, and now
that one routine had been established, there was something in
her that would have been quite happy just to continue the
same pattern, as if A. B. were still over in Korea. Estrangement was a more manageable thing than love. And yet what
could she do? He was her father and it was Christmas. And
there was no mistaking the tone of sincerity in his voice, the
ring of genuine repentance. Perhaps a miracle had indeed occurred, and the old man would learn to bite his tongue.

Oh, the power of Christmas for drawing together families,
those wiliest of enemies! There it sat in the dead of winter, a
pagan feast taken over by the Christians and then secularized,
a season both peaceful and tumultuous, garish and holy, in
which warring nations laid down their arms while families
took up knives and forks and sat down together to eat. People
who had hardly anything in common gathered around the
same holiday table in the soft glow of candles and colored
lights, to gnaw on the same carcass, to wear one another's

gifts, and to wrack their brains for something to talk about. Christmas was a kind of sacrament in which believer and unbeliever shared alike.

By the time the day arrived A. B.'s period of religious ecstasy had mysteriously passed. He knew it was over from the moment he laid eyes on the enormous plastic Santa Claus, complete with sleigh and reindeer, set up on the front lawn of Rita's house. He eyed it with the same disgust he had felt towards all those tawdry statues of the Buddha that littered the Far East. To A. B., Santa even bore some resemblance to the Buddha; both were roly-poly pig-men whose pasty faces gleamed with slovenly, self-satisfied smirks that people mistook for joy. No mere plastic effigy, this Santa Claus was an idol, a powerful alien god riding in a chariot. And like all idols he was an empty invention of man, a clay-footed means of sidestepping spiritual truth, of conveniently forgetting the one true Lord. He was a pagan leech who sucked glory away from Christ. For it was not Santa Claus who bestowed gifts at Christmas, it was the Lord Jesus. And as A. B. rang his daughter's doorbell that day he suddenly realized why it was that Santa wore a red suit—it was because he was the Devil in disguise!

Rita, teacher that she was, had decorated the whole house lavishly. There were lights inside and out, festoons of crepe paper, strings of popcorn, wreaths, mistletoe, and Christmas cards everywhere. A foil angel crowned the tree, A. B. noticed, but otherwise there was an obvious and studied avoidance of all religious symbols. Well, he had promised to say nothing. At least Rita was not averse to playing Christmas carols on the stereo, the kind of thing with "O Come All Ye Faithful" and "Here Comes Santa Claus" back to back, sung by a choir of orphan children.

Father and daughter embraced, but not without holding something back. Forgiveness, as it turned out, was not a business that could be transacted over the telephone. And when little Charlotte ran into his arms A. B.'s heart sank. Here was

a child who might never know the Lord! How could her
grandpa, on Christmas Day of all days, keep such a secret?
A. B. almost broke his resolve right then and there. As a
young man, before heading out to Korea, he had felt called to
take the gospel to the Muslims, but he had been thrown out
of two countries. He just did not possess the subtlety for such
a task. And now, he thought gloomily, being in his own
daughter's house was worse than trying to work with the
Muslims.

Yet somehow the day unfolded, with the opening of presents, the playing of games, a walk in the new snow. Between
Rita and her father there remained not an open coldness but a
formality, a stiffness that grew the more strained the harder
they sought to conceal it. Rattling on in their garrulous fashion, even guffawing over strings of queer jokes that no one
else would have caught, nevertheless beneath and behind it all
they watched one another, with gazes slow and wary, distant
as cats. Had it not been for Charlotte, the day would have
turned out a disaster. But she, thank God, behaved exactly as
a six-year-old child on Christmas Day ought to behave, bub-
bling around the adults like a tiny silver stream rushing
through a burnt-out woods. Her favorite present that day (it
happened also to be the most inexpensive) was a game of
pick-up sticks that A. B. had brought from Korea. It was the
Asian version, with the sticks made of ivory and ornately
carved in different patterns. For over an hour in the late afternoon, while Rita prepared supper, the girl and her grandfather stretched out on the living room floor and took turns
dropping the delicate white sticks in haphazard piles and then
picking them up again, using the one longer hooked piece to
extricate each stick one by one without disturbing any of the
others. It was a game requiring considerable coordination, and
while the old man's crooked bony hands trembled like aspen
leaves, Charlotte proudly held her pink and perfect fingers
rock steady, screwed up her face in histrionic concentration,
and deftly won game after game. Just being with the girl and

basking in her girlishness made A. B. relax more than he had all day. Parched places deep inside him were watered. Perhaps even for Charlotte the real game consisted less in winning than in seeing how long she could captivate her grandfather.

Finally it came time for Christmas dinner, a feast of feasts with both ham and turkey, potatoes and stuffing, three kinds of vegetable, and all the other trimmings. The food shone as if with its own inner light. There were crackers and special napkins, tall candles, and a red-and-green tablecloth. Rita had spared no effort. Yet as the three of them sat down to the glittering repast A. B. felt once again a sinking of the heart. Why so much food for just three people? And what good was such lavish external preparation if the heart also were not prepared? Could turkey, even a moist slab of breast with sweet crinkly skin, satisfy the soul? To top things off Rita did not even pause this evening for grace—a concession she had never denied her father in the past.

So, he thought, this was the way things would be. Even the little he had would be taken away. Again A. B. nearly broke his resolve. He thought of rising to his feet and praying to Jesus, crying out in the loudest voice he had. For a moment he let himself be mesmerized by a vision of the sheer melodrama of such an action. The whole meal would be ruined. Rita's sumptuous preparations would wither away into ashes, exposed in all their hollowness. Perhaps the very roof of the house would collapse upon them in judgement, and the plastic Santa Claus go up in smoke.

Just in time, however, A. B. caught himself. Was it zeal for the Lord's Name that moved him, or was it vindictiveness against his daughter? Swallowing his pride, therefore, and then a mouthful of turkey, he exclaimed, "Delicious! Best I've ever had! Rita, you're as fine a cook as your mother." He forced himself to be pleasant, talkative, even exuberant. But how hard it was. Whatever special outpouring of grace had buoyed him up during the past week, filling him with tenderness and new insight, it was gone now. The Lord had withdrawn His hand, and A. B. was on his own, left to love this rebellious daughter of his as best he could, in his own strength, and to express that love in an emasculated language, in words without vowels.

Halfway through the meal, predictably enough, even the thin protocol of politeness gave out, as an awkward and ponderous silence descended over the table. To A. B. it felt as though every possible avenue of conversation (except of course the gospel) had already been explored up and down twenty times, utterly exhausted, thrashed to living daylights. Every word now was like a heavy weight that had to be pulled up from the bottom of the sea. Even the chatterbox Charlotte was suddenly becalmed, and for what seemed an eternity the three of them sat there in the festive room as if all alone, each hopelessly cut off from the others. At the same time it was somehow as though there were a fourth presence with them at the table, invisible, yet mutely dominating the whole conversation. It was a presence like that of a prisoner in chains, allowed home for this one day in the year but destined to be returned to his cell by nightfall. Or perhaps it was like the presence of a senile elderly person whom the rest of the family had finally decided to crate up and ship off to a nursing home. It was a presence that cried out with reproach, shrieking like any ghost.

For an excruciating interlude there was no sound at all save breathing and chewing, the grim scraping of cutlery across plates, and the orphan choir grinding out "The Twelve Days of Christmas." Finally, just when the silent shrieking had grown almost unbearable, it was little Charlotte who spoke, who broke the deadlock. Gulping her milk, heaving a white-mustached sigh, and pointing her fork at A. B. like a microphone, she asked him pointblank, "Grandpa, why is today called Christmas?"

The child's question came like a peal of thunder. Out of the blue it fell crashing into the dining room just as though, indeed, the roof might be collapsing. For at that precise moment there could not have been a more dramatic occurrence if the plum pudding had exploded in the oven. Did the little girl have any idea what she was saying? Did she herself grasp, however dimly, the overwhelming significance of her question? Or was it possible that she was deliberately seeking to scandalize her elders? Did she sense the power she had over these two sullen adults, and would she now exploit it for all it was worth? Or was it the case that, like her grandfather, she wished merely to acknowledge the presence of the mysterious uninvited guest?

There was never any telling what lived in the mind of a child. But there it was, the mysterious question, and A. B. stopped his chewing, sighted along the silver shaft of the fork into his granddaughter's inscrutable blue eyes, and sincerely did not know what to say. To such a blunt question there was only one answer, a simple, clear, and precise answer. But he could not give it. He glanced down at Rita, as though asking permission to speak, but her face told him absolutely nothing. She looked as if she had just swallowed a small sharp bone but was not letting on. A. B. wrestled desperately with himself. Finally he just lowered his eyes to the table and said quietly, "Perhaps your mother could give you a better answer than I could."

And surprisingly, in his voice there were none of the shades and overtones of sarcasm he could easily have put there. There was no rancor, not the slightest quiver of irony, not even a hint of passing the buck. What came out, instead, like a bright flow of water emerging miraculously from a rock, was a tone of pure humility. The old man was simply defeated, tired of the struggle, utterly powerless. He had even given up blaming anyone.

Still Charlotte's question hung in the air. Or rather, the answer hung there, like one of the pinned ivory sticks in the game, a delicate white rod balanced precariously, which no one dared to touch. But now it was up to Rita; it was her move. And all at once, inside her too there was something that gave way, something that was defeated. It had been a trying day, and yet not nearly as trying for her as it had been for A. B. In fact, in spite of all the strain and the uncomfortable silence during supper, she had actually warmed to her father over the course of the afternoon. Never had she seen him so self-controlled and patient, so meek as he had been that day. It had rather awed her that this man who, she thought, would never change, had clearly changed.

And perhaps that is why, when finally she spoke, it was to say to her little daughter, "Today is called Christmas, Charlotte, because it is the birthday of Jesus Christ." And then she proceeded, despite a certain thickness in her voice, to give a brief explanation.

A. B. gawked at her. His own Rita was talking about the Lord! And was he mistaken, or was there actually a note of wonder in her voice, perhaps even the faintest hint of a reluctant reverance? After all, she might have made her reply with a cynical sneer. She might have answered haughtily, mordantly, perhaps with a little toss of her chin, as if to say, "Your grandfather worships this man, but you and I know better." Or she might simply have spoken flatly, matter-of-factly, as one does reciting statistics. But even that she did not do. No, instead into her answer had crept, just as it had into A. B.'s voice, a note of astonishing, of genuine, of radiant humility, something so unexpected that it caught even Rita off guard. Indeed she spoke almost as though she had just discovered the origins of Christmas herself, as if that very moment such knowledge had been revealed to her.

Tension, like a shamed animal, slunk out of the room. How it happened that sweeping transformations could follow in the wake of such minuscule developments, who could tell? But the effect was like that of driving out a demon. The plum pudding was carried in on a platter, as ceremoniously and triumphantly as if it were a haggis (for this was a sacred family tradition), and then A. B. put some brandy (of which he never touched a drop) into a spoon, warmed it over a candle until it ignited, and then poured the liquid fire over the nearly black pudding as the three of them leaned forward, their eyes shining, to watch it blaze. Laughter broke out again, Charlotte's face glowed like a little angel's, and the orphan choir started into "Silent Night."

There was no more talk of Jesus that evening. And yet, and yet—it was as if the Lord Himself, like a master goldsmith, had devised exactly the right setting in which the mere mention of His Name might shine forth like a spectacular jewel, like a diamond against a black velvet cloth.

Fiction and the Word

My heart is stirred by a noble theme
as I offer my verses to the King;
my tongue is the pen of a skillful writer.

—PSALM 45:1

A renowned professor of theology used to walk into his first class at the beginning of each semester and, before saying or doing anything else, hold the Bible aloft and proclaim, "This is *not* the Word of God. But it can *become* the Word of God in a receptive heart."

He was wrong, of course. It was like saying, "There is no God. But there can *become* a God wherever there is a human being gullible enough to believe in Him."

The fact of the matter is that the Word of God is the Word of God, whether anyone believes it or not. As the Lord Himself proclaims in Isaiah 55:10–11:

> As the rain and the snow
>   come down from heaven,
> and do not return to it
>   without watering the earth . . .
> so is My Word that goes out from My mouth:
>   It will not return to Me empty,
>   but will accomplish all that I desire.

The professor's problem was that he had rejected the Bible's own claim of being "God-breathed" (2 Tim. 3:16), choosing instead to regard it merely as a work of man-made literature. Inspired by God, perhaps, but not authored by Him. Not categorically different from many another book that has been spiritually "inspired."

If this man had been right, his point would have been a good one. For the problem with all man-made literature (including this present book) is that it is, indeed, *only words*. And man's words, while they hold the potential of *becoming* real, do not contain reality in themselves. Unlike the words of Jesus, which "will never pass away" (Matt. 24:35), the words of man will shrivel up like dead leaves and be whirled away in the wind. Be they spoken or written with the loftiest of intentions, in themselves they do not hold the power to water the earth (though often enough they succeed in parching it).

There is a story, dating from around the turn of the century, about a certain rich and cultured woman who enjoyed attending the theater. One winter night the play was a very powerful one, focusing on the theme of social inequality. For three hours this aristocrat sat in the warm theater and was profoundly moved, even to the point of tears, by the tragic plight of the poor as it was so vividly portrayed on the stage. Meanwhile throughout this performance the coachman who had driven his mistress to the theater sat outside on the open box of her carriage, huddling against the cold while keeping an eye on the horse in the shafts. When finally the elegant woman emerged from her moving theater experience, was she in turn moved to see her poor coachman all covered with snow and shivering? Not at all. She simply accepted the scene as part of the ordinary and unchanging routine of her life.

Of course such complacency was not necessarily the fault of the play. Rather, it was the fault of the woman's own cold heart. (Even the Bible can, and often does, leave people cold.) But in contrast to this tale, there is a lovely story entitled "The Most Beautiful Player of All," contained in the fine book *Tales of the Resistance* by David and Karen Mains (Elgin, IL: Chariot Books, 1986). Here, in the middle of a performance of one in a myth-cycle of plays called "The Return of the King," starring a famous and beloved actress, there is a sudden power failure. All at once the entire theater is plunged into darkness, and the enchantment of the play's art is momentarily broken. Yet in that very juncture of surprise intermission, who should appear out of the shadows and vault up onto the stage . . . but the King Himself! No actor, but *Jesus* in person! It is a stupendous moment, as the Lord of lords, bearing His own inimitable radiance, stands before both actors and audience and with arms outspread announces, "There is a *real* Kingdom, and a *real* King!"

Is this not exactly what needs to happen in any truly Christian work of literature? At some point the spell of the art itself must be broken, as it were, in order to allow for the Lord Jesus Himself to make an appearance. This is also, incidentally, what absolutely *must* happen in every church service; and yet it is precisely what all too many church services resist like the plague. But if the Church shuns her Lord's real presence, is it any wonder if art and literature also resist the grand entrance of the Lord Jesus, just as though His presence there would be a plague upon them?

In "The Ghost of Christmas," does Jesus put in a personal appearance? I like to think so. It's the only reason I wrote it, the only reason I write anything. All that vain spilling of ink is utterly worthless to me, except as a lowly means of *setting up*, or *inviting*, the possibility of Incarnation, the possibility of a real manifestation of Christ within the pages of a book and so, hopefully, in the life of some anonymous reader. This is a long shot, some might say, and attended by an absurd vanity. For can my artificial art really become a vehicle for the living God? Can my mere *words* be transformed into Word? But I leave that to Him. It's His job to appear. It's my job to pray, to hope, to write—and to write, indeed, as though my life depended upon it, as though all my ink were a spillage of blood, and all for the sake of Christ.

Certainly the one thing I find most terribly frustrating about the craft of fiction (and probably about the daily living of the Christian life as well) is what a tremendous amount of sheer legwork must be done simply in order to facilitate this incarnational event. What an enormous volume of words must be written, scenes and characters created, and ink, sweat, tears, and blood spilled just in order to earn the right to name the Name of Jesus, to speak into an unbelieving world the real and transforming presence of its own Creator! Just like old A. B. in my story, I keep asking myself: why should such a right have to be earned at all?

But there is no way around it. People will read fiction who would never be caught dead reading or listening to a sermon. And inevitably such readers turn out to be the sort who read with a desperate, an unholy, a carcinogenic voracity. They read like elephants munching peanuts. A paragraph that might have taken me three days to write is to this audience like one grain of salt on the skin of one peanut. A hundred pages of close print means nothing at all to such bookworms. They are print-oholics, addicts who in many cases have reached the point where their compulsive habit does not even provide them with true pleasure anymore.

That is why it is so important to me, in everything I write, to go for the jugular. A Christian writer of fiction has no time for fooling around, even if the actual daily practice of the craft, together with the result, may often appear like nothing *but* fooling around. But Franz Kafka was so right: "If the book we are reading does not wake us, as with a fist hammering on our skull, why then do we read it? . . . A book must be an ice-axe to break the sea frozen inside us." Such eloquent, much-quoted words these are, and yet the Christian cannot help but question whether they really apply to anything Kafka himself wrote. For when asked his opinion of Christ, the Wielder of the one true ice-axe, Kafka gave an answer that is as honest and admirable as it is damning: "He is an abyss filled with light; one must close one's eyes if one is not to fall in."

So yes, I like to think that somehow in the writing I do there are moments of real Incarnation, moments when it becomes possible for the reader to fall into the abyss of light, with eyes wide open. And I'm convinced that such moments are accomplished not through the power of fiction, essentially, nor through any obvious display of spirituality, necessarily, but rather through the Holy Spirit of God at work in a few simple, homely, worldly props: a Christmas dinner, a little girl's awkward question, a father and a daughter who simultaneously love and hate one another.

As with two other stories in this book ("Bound For Glory" and "The Changeling"), the story of Rita, Charlotte, and A. B. was originally written as something to send out to our personal friends at Christmas time in place of a store-bought greeting card. This is a tradition I've followed for several years now, and always the challenge God sets before me is that of trying by His grace alone to impart, into a jumble of mere words, some moment of *Christophany*, some instant in which the Ghost of Christmas Himself, shining by His own radiance rather than by that of my art, puts in an appearance on the darkened stage.

This is a loftier ambition, please note, than that of simply "writing a good story," or being a good artist. For to quote Thomas Merton again, commenting on his own father, "The integrity of an artist lifts a man above the level of the world without delivering him from it." So my aim is much higher than merely the "common grace" with which God can fill any work of art, even the works of pagans. No, the petition I offer before the throne of grace is this: that my words, even though they are not the Word of God, might nevertheless *become* the Word of God in receptive hearts. Will the Lord of Glory grant me such grace? Will He bestow on me, to some small extent, a portion of that grace He gave to the prophet Samuel, of whom it was said (astonishingly) that God "let none of his words fall to the ground" (1 Sam. 3:19)?

But yes, no less than that is my constant prayer for my writing. It is much the same prayer that all secular artists offer to their own imaginations, or else to the god of Art or to one of a bewildering pantheon of muses and *daimons*. But the Psalmist offers it to the Lord, the Maker of Heaven and Earth, pleading, "Establish the work of my hands, O Lord; by all means, establish the work of my hands!" (Ps. 90:17) And I too offer my prayer to the only God who is able to answer it. In the words of my own freewheeling writer's paraphrase of Psalm 137:4–6:

> How shall I sing of the Kingdom of God
>   in the alien land of literature?
> If I ever forget Thee in my books, Lord Jesus,
>   then let my right hand forget how to write!
> If I do not extol Thee in all my work,
>   then please, please, reduce me to silence!
> Yes—may I never write again
>   if I do not count Christ my greatest joy!

Priit Laas

People are always introducing me to other writers. They assume, I suppose, that we'll have things in common, when the fact of the matter is that writers seldom see eye to eye. "Two of the same trade never agree," observed Thoreau, and loneliness and staunch individualism are an author's stock-in-trade. Literary people can socialize, and they can chat about books, critics, and word processors, but I for one have never quite been able to share my heart with another writer. For that I seem to need someone so far removed from my work as to pose no personal threat. Writers are an arrogant, insecure, small-minded breed, and if anything true or good happens to spill out of them onto paper, it is generally by accident, the accident of grace.

Some time ago my wife and I decided to spend a year in a small town in the interior of British Columbia. We arranged to trade houses with a doctor there who wanted to take some courses in the city. My wife would fill in for him, and I had a novel to begin. "You'll love it here," our friend told us. "I can't think of a more perfect place to write a book—unless you were to go to an island in the Aegean. In fact, we even have our own resident author here, a wonderful old fellow. You'll have lots to talk about, I'm sure. And there's a great curling club too. You won't get bored, I can tell you that much."

Though we had driven through the town many times, we knew it only for its dreary string of restaurants and gas stations. But the day we arrived, a Saturday in September, it was one of those magical autumn afternoons when the sun is so splendid it seems to come right down out of the sky and illuminate from within everything it touches. All the buildings shone cleanly and mysteriously as things do at night, and even the streets looked burnished, golden. The house we were to occupy was beside a rushing mountain river, and as soon as we got out of the car we went straight down to the water and gazed at it incredulously. The river was clear as a window and spangled with froth and the sound of it filled our ears like the sound of all the leaves falling off all the trees all at once. Having no heart for unpacking just then, we hiked a short way up the mountainside to a point of lookout. Our little tumbling river came down to meet a much broader, rolling one, and there sat the town, at the junction of the two rivers, with mountains humped all around like huge, dark, shining clouds anchored to the earth. The air was blue as water but perfectly transparent, and the two arms of the valley spread out into the azure distance like wings.

On Sunday morning when we went to church, the sky was overcast. There was a choice between United, Pentecostal, or Lutheran, so we opted for Lutheran. It was a white frame building, very plain, and so high and narrow it seemed almost to be standing on its end. Sitting inside, one got the satisfying impression of being in the hold of a ship. Metal cables and braces held the structure together, and colorful banners hung down from the roof, some printed with sayings in an unfamiliar language. Others declared "God is our refuge and strength" or, "worship the Lord in the beauty of holiness," and they were quilted with golden trumpets, blue and red angels, stars and doves. They were simple but by far the most beautiful things in the building. The church was only about half full. The service was short and formal, and the minister preached a correct but lackluster sermon. The people kept their coats on. My wife and I sat in a pew by ourselves and wondered, as we always do in a strange church, whether there were any Christians here.

Afterwards we had coffee. A tiny, vivacious woman, silver-haired and hardly bigger than a child, took us under her wing and showed us into the hall, somehow managing to chatter continuously while still finding out all about us. Such people are the backbone of any congregation. When she asked what I did for a living, I replied, "My wife is a doctor," a stock answer that normally absolves me from any further explanation. But of course my wife was right there to blurt out the whole truth, and when the woman learned that I was a writer her silver eyebrows shot up and she exclaimed, "You don't say!" suddenly letting out all her breath as if she'd been punctured. Then, pursing her lips and giving me a look replete with meaning, she said, "Well, you *must* come and meet Mr. Priit Laas. He's a writer too!" And fastening onto my elbow, she steered me across the room.

An elderly man was sitting on a chair in the corner, and the first thing I noticed was that he had a white cane and a bushy head of snow-white hair with a matching mustache that put me in mind of Mark Twain. The face was much gentler, though, long and delicately featured. His eyes bulged slightly and were milky with cataracts, but behind the mist I could see that they were a beautiful pale green, at once reflective and penetrating, with crinkles of good humor at the corners. He was dressed in a dark suit and looked straight ahead, his hands clasped over the head of the cane. Somehow, even before he said a word, I felt that I liked him, although I also decided instantly that he would be the compiler of the local history book, or the sort of man who publishes lighthearted verse on the editorial page of the weekly newspaper.

Our little woman was so pleased to be bringing two writers together that she neglected to mention my name. She simply announced, "Mr. Laas, this man is a *writer*," giving the word every conceivable overtone of significance.

"Ah," said Priit Laas. "Well, well. And you're a Lutheran too? That's a fine combination."

I tried to explain that I was not really a Lutheran, but that I hoped we would fit in.

"Well, you're certainly welcome," he said. "Denomination means nothing. All that counts is to be head over heels in love with Jesus."

There was no proselytizing brashness in his tone. He spoke simply and smiled not just with his mouth but with his whole face. Even behind the cataracts his eyes seemed to have a perpetual twinkle. Normally I am a shy person with strangers, but this man put me at ease. Though I'd never noticed it before, it can be very relaxing being in the presence of the blind and knowing one is invisible. An element of pressure, of judgment, is eliminated. In no time at all the two of us fell into an intimate conversation about our faith. I found it strange not to be looking around the room to see who else there was to talk to. Priit Laas was a man of firm but humble belief who also appeared to be widely read in theology. He made references to Bonhoeffer, Kirkegaard, and Karl Barth. He quoted Martin Luther, who apparently had claimed to be so busy that he couldn't possibly get everything done unless he spent at least three hours each day in prayer. All the while we talked, Priit Laas's eyes wrinkled at the corners and shone behind their clouds of cataract. Several times he laughed with such gusto that his head bobbled around and it seemed his white hair might all blow away like a crown of dandelion seeds. As he said not a word about writing, finally it was I who broached the subject, asking him the one question I myself always cringe to hear.

"Tell me, what sort of writing do you do?"

"Oh, a little poetry," he answered. "An occasional essay or translation. But *fiction*—" He sighed. "That's where my heart really is. Fiction is my great love." But here we were interrupted, and that was all he said.

When it came time to go, Priit Laas gave me a card with his name on it, and I asked him about the peculiar spelling. He told me he was Estonian, and I was surprised to learn that

most of the people in the church were also of Estonian de-
scent, together with about a third of the community. I had to
confess that I had only the vaguest idea of what an Estonian
was and that I didn't think I'd ever met one before.

"There aren't many of us," Priit reflected. "Even in the
homeland nearly half of the present population is non-Estoni-
an. But then everyone in the world is in a minority, don't you
think?"

On the way home I told my wife all about my conversation
with the blind Estonian Christian writer. I found myself keen-
ly curious now about his work. Somehow I felt certain it
would be good, profound, true. He had such a deep and genuine faith, and indeed his whole character rang true, glowed
with authenticity. The words wisdom and humility sprang to
my mind. Such a man would not be a hack. I had really been
quite moved by my contact with him. How peculiar it was to
come all the way out here to this remote village and on the
second day to meet the sort of person I had given up on ever
meeting, a person who simply did not exist in the city. Of
course I was acquainted with many Christian writers. Most of
them were poets, and there were a few prose writers who
specialized in fantasy or science fiction. All of which was fine.
The gospel could be accommodated easily enough to such
forms. But serious realistic fiction (which was my area) was a
different matter. There was a handful of people who wrote in
this genre and called themselves Christians, but to my mind
they were Christians only in the intellect. Some of them were
truly brilliant writers, yet from the standpoint of faith I felt
that their writing was dead. They exploited Christianity for its
symbolic power, but there was no real presence of the Holy
Spirit in such works. In fact, reading them, I always had the
impression that they were ashamed even to mention the name
of Jesus, except as a swear word. Fiction and the Christian
faith, it was commonly assumed, mixed like oil and water. Religion was propaganda, and literature abhorred propaganda.

These thoughts came tumbling out as I talked over with my wife the meeting with Priit Laas. She, as it turned out, had been introduced to Mrs. Laas and had been equally intrigued. Friida was a quiet, gentle woman who exuded an aura of strength, of having been victorious over many trials. She had quilted the beautiful banners in the church, and both she and her husband were apparently fine pianists.

We felt honored, therefore, when a few days later Friida phoned and invited us to supper. The Laases lived in a small bungalow on the mountainside, and we arrived just as dusk was falling, with the mountains dark and crude like children's cut-outs against the luminous sky. Friida met us at the door and escorted us into the living room, where Priit was sitting with the lights out, his white head of hair forming the brightest spot in the semi-darkness. He told us he loved this time of twilight, and we sat there with him in front of a magnificent picture window while he pointed things out to us as if he could still see them. The jewelled town lay below like a distant galaxy in the black folds of the valley, while the sky seemed a more radiant blue than it ever was at noon.

"You see that tiny cluster of lights far up the valley?" he said. "There's a gold mine there. This whole country still crawls with prospectors. And if you look directly across the river, just above the mountain, you should be able to see Venus. It will be almost exactly in the center of that little cleft just below the highest peak. It should be there right now."

Sure enough, Venus was there, splendidly bright, and after a few minutes we watched it wink out behind the peak. Priit got us to tell him the exact moment when it disappeared, and what it looked like as it crashed silently against the mountain and ignited one single tree, as if in a burst of flames, just before vanishing. He seemed to take enormous pleasure in viewing the event through our eyes and helping us to see it. He knew a good deal about astronomy, and he seemed to have the whole geography of the valley and the precise silhouette of each mountain etched into his mind.

"I knew for a long time that I was losing my sight," he told us, "and I set about deliberately to memorize things. Or perhaps every writer does that anyway. But even as a child I looked hard, hard, at the world, filing away images, as if already I knew that the night was coming, the time when everything would be swallowed up and there would be no more looking. What is it Ecclesiastes says? 'The eye never has enough of seeing.' But I've done my seeing, and perhaps I see things better now."

We learned that Priit's blindness was due not to cataracts but to diabetes, the "brittle" form of the disease that was so hard to control. For years he had been in and out of hospitals, and there had been no end of ugly complications. Yet all of this he mentioned only in passing, and not until Friida called us into supper did I begin to realize the full extent of Priit's sickness. For he got out of his chair like a man struggling against an enormous invisible weight. He used two canes for walking and took only tiny steps. He was surprisingly tall, but he walked like a toddler. His legs jerked in little spasms as if they were being moved by puppet strings, and I noticed then how wasted his whole body appeared, shrunken and emaciated. Brittle was exactly the word for the way he looked, and it seemed as though he might collapse at any moment, caving in right through the floor and leaving behind nothing but a pile of clothes. As long as he had remained seated, one was drawn in and held by those extraordinary eyes of his. The eyes of the blind are always strangely arresting, and his were riveting. But as he painstakingly wobbled to his feet and traversed those few steps into the dining room, I looked into his face again and saw what I had not seen before—agony, and the skin stretched tight as bone itself. Underneath the great head of snowy hair and the bushy mustache he was little more than a shadow, a shadow with beautiful apple-green eyes that looked out as if from another body.

After supper we drank strong coffee and the Laases talked of Estonia. Both had been separated from their families during the war. Priit's father, a professor of literature, had been one of ten thousand intellectuals rounded up by the Russians in a single night in 1941.

"He simply disappeared," Priit related. "All I know is he was dragged from his bed at midnight and four Russian soldiers marched him out of the house. He was still in pajamas, red polka-dot ones, when I last saw him. Of course I never heard for sure, but I presume he was stuffed into a freight car and shipped off to a labor camp east of the Urals. It sounds banal even to describe this, since the same fate befell so many. But perhaps that is the most terrible thing of all about suffering—the banality of it. I might as well tell you what my father ate for breakfast; it would be more interesting. But after the Russians came the Germans, and then it was the Russians again. The Germans were atrocious, but the Russians were worse. People disappeared, and if you asked why, you were taken yourself. Do you know that during the forties 350,000 Estonians were lost—a third of the population? Vanished. Poof!—like smoke. I have lost my eyes, but these people were swallowed whole into the earth. You will look in vain for their tombstones."

Priit had joined the resistance movement known as the Forest Brothers. But when the Red Army pushed back the Germans in 1944 he, together with thousands of others, fled for the borders. He was lucky enough to hop onto a ship headed for Danzig, and the very next day the gate slammed shut on Estonian emigration. For Priit there followed four years in a displaced persons' camp in Germany, where he met and married Friida. It was just when they were finally accepted into Canada that the diabetes took hold with a series of violent episodes, leading ultimately to diabetic coma.

"He nearly died," recalled Friida. "It was very frightening, more so than anything we had yet experienced."

"It was the best thing that could have happened," Priit interrupted. "On my own I would never have had the courage to set up as a writer. As a university student in Tallinn I had dreamed of writing, but even then I could barely sit still long enough to write a sentence. But the Lord showed me how to sit still. He made it so I couldn't do anything else. He knows what He's doing."

Friida listened quietly and spent the whole evening knitting. She looked as though she had been born knitting. She reminded me of my grandmother, who had knitted one pair of socks every day throughout the war and continued the practice right up until the day she died thirty years later. Friida, too, knit as if lives depended on it. When we left that night she stood in the doorway and whispered to me, "It means a great deal to my husband to have another writer to talk to."

We saw the Laases frequently after that, and although we talked often about books somehow the specific topic of writing seldom came up between us. I took this as a good sign, deciding that Priit must be aware of one of the great secrets of writing—that to talk about one's work was to lose the energy for actually doing it. Still, I grew more and more curious. To my mind this man was clearly no dilettante, and I would not have been surprised if someone had told me that he was a top-ranking Estonian author. From the few comments he did make I knew that he worked hard at his desk every day, whenever he was healthy enough, from morning until early afternoon. He wrote in Estonian on a braille typewriter, and Friida transcribed all his work.

One Sunday I got talking again to the tiny silver-haired woman at our church, and I tried to find out more about Priit's reputation.

"Oh yes, he's extremely well known," she said quickly. Her voice was just like a piccolo. "You'll often see one of his stories in our Estonian quarterly magazine. But I don't suppose you read Estonian, do you?"

Before long the Laases invited us to join them in a weekly Bible-study group that met in their home. There were two other couples, and we grew accustomed to sitting with these people in the beautiful front room with the picture window that looked out over the town, and praying and discussing the Scriptures together. I was frequently moved by Priit's insights and his prayers. "Faith is being certain of what we do not see," wrote the author of Hebrews, and it really seemed to me at times that Priit had his blind eyes fixed on what the rest of us only glimpsed. Often we sang hymns, and Priit accompanied us on the piano. Friida had the more polished technique, but Priit could play wonderfully by ear, and seated at the big upright grand, his lanky, sick body took on new vigor, blending into the music just the way Friida did into her knitting. Occasionally he played for sing-alongs at the church, and every Sunday he read the lessons. He and Friida would sit in the front pew, but still it was a considerable effort for him to heave himself out of his seat and to climb the three steps up to the lectern. The strain of this would leave him gasping for breath quite desperately, like a drowning sailor just plucked from the sea, and so he would begin his trek long in advance, leaving plenty of time to recover himself before reading. Then, staring straight ahead, he would translate the braille text into a voice so sonorous and melodious that even for the listener the words became almost palpable.

As well as being active in the church, Priit was very involved in community work. He visited at the hospital and sat on the board, he was a member of the Rotary Club and the Historical Society, and he was often invited to speak at various functions throughout the valley. Once a month Friida drove him into the city, where they stayed overnight and spent a day attending meetings of an Estonian cultural society. He seemed to be always busy. Only once did I have a chance to go into his study, in search of a book on prayer that he wanted to loan me, and then I was amazed at the piles and piles of manuscripts. There were several filing cabinets, but apparently even these were not enough to hold all the projects Priit was working on. Books, many of them Estonian titles, lined all four walls. The only name familiar to me was that of

Eduard Vilde, although I knew nothing about his writing, nor even that he was Estonian.

"Do you realize," Priit told me, "that in fiction alone there are now over one hundred Estonian-language titles being published every year?"

I asked him then what works of his own had been among that number.

"Nay, nay, you mistake me," he replied, shaking his head and laughing. "I am not an author, only a writer, a scribbler. The world takes no interest in my work. I've published a few stories and poems, that's all."

His voice trailed off. For the first time I thought that his smile looked tense, artificial. The question of publishing can be a delicate one for a writer. It is almost like asking a man's age or how much money he earns. And the world is so full of writers who have neither money nor published books, but only age to show for all their pains. Still, I found it difficult to comprehend how a man of Priit's character, both gifted and hard-working, could have met with no success. I wondered if he were being modest. Who else but a genius could possess in a sick body such incredible vitality? His flesh was exhausted, hanging by a few threads, but his spirit burned like a torch. Where did he get all the energy? All I knew was that he put me to shame. Three or four hours of writing finished me for the day. After that I was good for nothing except poking around town, reading, taking a quiet walk, or maybe chopping a bit of wood for the stove. For me writing and then recovering in order to write again the next day made for a full-time job.

Occasionally after my stint of work I liked to go to the coffee shop of the motor hotel, a local hangout. There I would order a cup of coffee and pretend to read a newspaper while listening in on the conversations of the miners and loggers, the businessmen and railroad workers. One afternoon, just as I got settled, who should come in but Priit Laas? Immediately two burly men jumped up to hold open the door for him, and a chorus of greetings issued from all over the room. Everyone in the place seemed to know him. Laboriously he made his way to a table in the center of the room, and by the time he finally collapsed into a chair he was dreadfully out of breath, bent double and wheezing.

A trucker named Henry was at the table, and reaching across and giving Priit's hair a playful tussle, he asked, "What keeps you going, Priit, old boy?"

Without missing a beat Priit responded, "Eternity, Henry, eternity.".

As he looked up I saw that his face was beaming, bright with pain but also with joy, the two held in an impossible fusion. He seemed almost to be laughing at his own misery. As there was an empty chair I joined the two men, and just at that point the waitress came up.

"You look like you could use a coffee, Mr. Laas," she said.

"Can I just get a breath of air?" he quipped. "A little fresh oxygen? Or how about a pint of blood?"

Then he made a joke to me, something about writers and coffee shops, all the while looking as if he might choke. He had just come from the library, it turned out—a distance of three blocks. Twice a week Friida drove him downtown to the library, and when he was finished there he would walk up to the hotel by himself for coffee, and there she would pick him up.

"You hear wonderful stories here," he told me. "In the church you hear gossip, but here you find out what's really going on in the world. There's a short story in every cup of coffee."

With Henry present there was no more mention of writing, and not until we got up to leave did Priit take me aside and tell me a surprising piece of news. He was very near, he said, to completing a long manuscript, a translation of all his Estonian short stories into English. He had worked at the project off and on for several years, but lately he'd been pouring all his time into it because, he said, he particularly wanted to show the work to me and to get my reactions. He referred to this as his magnum opus, a book more dear to him than any of his novels. He was hoping it would be the work that might gain him some notice among English readers. He still had several weeks of editing to do. But when it was finished, would I look it over, he asked, and give him a good hard criticism?

"I want you to be tough on me," he emphasized. "No fooling around. I have no shortage of friends who will smile pleasantly and tell me how wonderful my writing is. But the publishers, for some reason they do not smile. So from you I want criticism. I do not want to know what is good about the writing, only what is bad, only what needs to be changed."

Naturally I replied I would be honored to read his work. The fact that it had been rejected by publishers did not prejudice me in the least but on the contrary intrigued me all the more. For I had already decided that his difficulties were probably a result of his Christian faith. Religious fiction was not in vogue. I knew all about such troubles myself, and I wondered whether I might even be of some help in getting my friend's work into the right hands. I suppose I began to imagine myself as the "discoverer" of Priit Laas. For I had gone so far as to form a secret hope, even an intuition, that this might be a man who had found a voice for some of the very things I myself was struggling to express. One could hunger for such a writer more than for food and search ravenously through bookstores and libraries and fall almost into despair over being apparently the only person in the world who saw things in a certain light. But then, that was the very motive for writing in the first place: an insatiable hunger existed for a sort of book that was not available in any bookstore or library, since it had not yet been written. A reader would search and search until, in a passion of longing, he arrived at the realization that he himself must write the missing volume, the one book that could explain himself to himself. That was the way good books were born, out of desperate loneliness. And oddly enough perhaps it was this very hunger for a true soul mate that had the effect of isolating writers, cutting them off from one another. For the human craving for intimacy far outstripped its capacity to be met by other people.

It was that same afternoon, after returning from the coffee shop, that my wife spread out the latest copy of the local newspaper in front of me, and there on the editorial page was a poem by Priit Laas, printed in both Estonian and English. I read it through eagerly, then more slowly. But I was disappointed. It was a patriotic piece called "My Fatherland," with a few good lines and images, but a few bad ones too. There were "flowery meadows" and "dusky pines," and the "heart yearned" for such things. Well, I reflected, it had probably lost a lot in the translation. There was never any telling with translations of poetry. Besides, a truly good writer of fiction was certainly allowed, if he liked, to turn out a few undistinguished poems.

Very early that autumn a bitter cold set in. The townspeople said it couldn't last, but it did, right through the winter without a break. By the first week in November there were already thick shelves of ice along both banks of our little river. The water was so fast moving that it was incredible to think it could freeze over at all, and every day I went out to watch for a few minutes, to see how the mystery happened. Even in the swiftest parts of the current, I saw, there were lazy eddies and dark pools. There the ice gripped first, and once it had a foothold it would act as a dam, creating more and more backwaters and pools that in turn would succumb to freezing. The whole process was like the advance of an army or a disease. Each day I could see the river growing more sluggish. Floes formed, then backed up, until even the open water began to take on a frozen look, slivered with crystals, blue with cold, a barely moving slurry. The sound of the river changed from day to day, becoming first like a great forest of clinking wind chimes and then like slush sliding through a straw. One morning I went out early and there was no sound at all. The

entire torrent had been stopped dead in its tracks. There was
an unearthly silence, almost like a faint sound in itself, as if
the open river still roared through some ghostly chasm far beneath the earth.

It was a cold, still evening that December when Friida came
by the house and delivered Priit's manuscript of short stories.
It was an enormously fat thing, higher than it was wide.
Three manila folders had been taped together and tied around
it with thick twine. It had the weight of a cinder block. I set it
on the table for a few moments and simply marveled. Sometimes it was possible to fall in love with a book even before
opening it. It was as if the object itself emanated an aura as
powerful and distinctive as that of the person behind it. At
the same time, gazing at Priit's accomplishment, I became
aware of the irrational fear that someone else might have accomplished my own life's work ahead of me.

My wife was on call that night at the hospital and would
probably be busy for the whole evening. Carefully I un-
wrapped the manuscript and laid it on the arm of my favorite
reading chair. Then I put on the coffee pot and built a good
fire in the stove. Everything was as luxurious as if I had been
a king in a palace. Despite my strange fear I felt the sumptuous anticipation of a man about to make love. Through the
living room window I could see stars. Orion was standing
right on top of the nearest mountain, as if he too peered
down expectantly into the sheaf of pages before me.

The stories in the collection were arranged chronologically
according to date of composition, and so I did what I would
not normally do: I began at the beginning. The first few, fore-
seeably, were less than satisfying, and it wasn't long before I
flipped to the middle of the manuscript. Yet even then I
couldn't seem to get into these stories. I found myself skim-
ming, reading beginnings and endings or only the dialogue.
Finally I turned to the last piece, really a novella, and determined to give it a fair reading. But halfway through I set the
book down, got up and paced the room, stood at the window,

bit the nail of my thumb. The stars were still there, but they had grown lifeless, unreal. Orion was tipped on his side, sliding down the western slope of the mountain.

Without reading another word I knew that I did not like Priit's stories. I didn't like them at all. They were outlandish tales of bizarre characters—bums, adventurers, kings, minstrels, philosophers—set in a mythical town located somewhere between dream and reality. It was a sort of Greenwich Village of the Dark Ages, and the characters lived out (or in) their fantasies. Sex, violence, and all sorts of perversions, while not always explicit, were everywhere hinted at and joked about, and free use was made of four-letter words. It was the sort of writing that an admiring critic might have labeled "exuberant," "boisterous," "rippling with gusto," or "magical." But it left me cold. There were ten times as many words as necessary. The sentences went on and on, rhapsodically. It was unabashedly melodramatic. It reminded me of the writing of Thomas Wolfe, which as a youth I had adored but which now I couldn't stomach. The most conspicuous virtue was that the characters were so lifelike they jumped off the page. Yet at the same time it was clear that Priit, unlike Wolfe, was not drawing at all on autobiographical material. Quite evidently the stuff had all come gushing straight out of his imagination. Nowhere did he explore the material of Estonia, for example, or the war, or anything to do with his own blindness or diabetes. Stranger still, and to my mind more troubling, was the total absence of any concern for Christian values. It wasn't just the vulgar language or the fact that the name of God was never once mentioned. That was only the tip of the iceberg. On a deeper level it seemed to me, as was the case with so much modern literature, that no lasting values were portrayed at all, no truths proclaimed, no judgment passed. Tenderness, brutality, love, insanity—all were present at once, all rolled up into one enthusiastically reported wad of passion. "Life" was "celebrated," from a stance that as far as I could see was utterly amoral.

I couldn't understand this. I couldn't accept it. I could barely believe this was the work of the wise and godly man I
knew. Pouring myself another cup of coffee, I sat down with
the book once again to read a few more of the later stories.
But no, they were the same all the way through. No one could
have guessed from such writing that the author was the least
bit interested in Jesus Christ, let alone loved Him.

It was after midnight when my wife came home, and by
then I was as crestfallen as if I myself had written this disillu-
sioning tome. I could scarcely open my mouth to tell her
about it.

"What am I going to do?" I wailed. "I can't possibly say to
him what I really think!"

"Didn't he ask you to be hard on him?"

"Sure, but that's only because he thinks his stuff is good.
He's hoping for the sort of criticism that will help him to
tighten it up a little. But how do you tighten up a mountain
of self-indulgent garbage?"

"Isn't there something constructive you can say?"

"Not without lying through my teeth."

The next morning I reluctantly set aside my own writing to
spend the day preparing a detailed, constructive criticism of
several of Priit's stories. Yet where to begin? Trying my best to
think objectively, I had to admit the writing was competent.
Good enough, in fact, that I honestly wondered why Priit had
had no success in getting it published, even in Estonian.
There were obvious weaknesses, but there was also brilliance.
There was even the occasional sentence or whole paragraph so
perfect that it made me wish I had written it myself.

Even so, how could I pretend to make literary evaluations
when my underlying problem was not literary at all but religious? It was the one problem you were not allowed to have
in discussions of literature or any of the arts, even though in
practice the bottom line for every critic, I was convinced, was
always ideology, not artistic merit. This was particularly true
when it came to contemporary literature. Secretly the critic

either accepted or rejected the ideological assumptions of the work in question, and then he took it from there. That was how people judged other people, and that was also how they judged art. The essential, though surreptitious, task of criticism was to find artistic grounds for justifying tastes and preferences that were secretly moral, philosophical, or religious. It was simply the way the game was played.

Sulkily I wracked my brains for diplomatic comments to make about Priit's manuscript. I praised his characterization to the skies, but suggested small plot changes and made minor, token corrections. Selecting half a dozen of the purpler passages, I gave them a quick editing. It was agonizing work. My problem was not with one or two loaves but the whole batch of dough. Years before I had made a solemn resolution never to encourage writing that did not genuinely move me. Better to risk losing a friendship than to do that. But life, it seemed, had a way of militating against solemn resolutions. Priit Laas was a friend I truly respected, a person I had even grown to love. He was a brother in Christ. And besides all that, he was twice my age; he'd been writing before I was born. And he was a sick man who thrived on his work. Who was I to pull out the rug from under him?

Eventually, mulling these things over, I decided upon a strategy. While I did not think I had the heart to confront Priit with my true feelings about his work, what I could do, perhaps, gently but firmly, was to try to steer him towards a different kind of writing altogether, perhaps something closer to home. For why, I wondered, did he seem to be avoiding all that was most personal to him? If there were any secret to writing, I felt, it lay in the author identifying his own authentic subject matter, hearing his own voice. If I could somehow nudge Priit in this direction—towards a more frank exploration of his own suffering, for example—it might prove to be the very encouragement he needed.

A few days later I arranged to meet him at his house. I was able to walk across our solidly frozen little river to a path that wound its way through the woods on the opposite bank all the way down to the junction with the other river, a distance of about two miles. Though this river appeared to be slower moving it was wider and deeper and had not frozen over completely. Between uncertain shelves of ice a broad band of current still slid darkly along in the middle, smooth as combed hair and tinted a deep translucent green like old glass. For a while I sat on the bank, pondering the way light and dark were mixed together in the water, and then I found the trail leading up the mountainside to where Priit lived.

When I arrived the two of us went into the kitchen and I watched silently as his hands measured out the coffee, poured cream, found cups and spoons. Supporting himself against countertops, he moved at once deftly and stiffly, seeming to combine perfect naturalness with a pained concentration. Although his characteristic expression was a crinkly smile, now and then I would glimpse the anguish among the crinkles. Yet his eyes shone with a pure light. How could there be such brightness in them? I wondered. I thought of that odd saying of Jesus, "The eye is the lamp of the body."

Taking our coffee, we went into the front room and proceeded to spend an hour going over some of the notes I had made about Priit's manuscript. Although I did not say so directly I found myself conveying the impression that his stories were wonderful, nearly perfect, requiring just a little more work to become true masterpieces. As my prevarication increased in complexity I grew more and more restless. I was remembering a chance comment Priit himself had once made to me, concerning Dostoevsky's character Alyosha in *The Brothers Karamozov*. "What I like about him," he had said, "is that he invariably tells the truth, the most difficult and the most dangerous thing in the world to do." This remark now lodged in my gullet, and I felt myself filling up with resentment as though Priit himself were twisting a knife in me, forcing me to be dishonest about his work. Finally, when I could stand this no longer, I pushed the manuscript to one side.

"Priit," I said, "your stories are marvelous, magical. But I have to tell you there is one thing about them that rather perplexes me. I'm not sure how to say this . . . But why isn't there more of, well, *yourself*? Why isn't there more of Priit Laas in your writing?"

Priit cocked his head to one side and made a quizzical face. "More of myself?" he asked. He looked like a child feigning incomprehension.

"Yes," I went on. "What I mean is, why don't you draw more on the concrete material of your own personal experience? Why this preposterous, mythical setting? Why nothing about your struggles with illness, for example, or about what it's like to go blind? Why nothing about the war, or about your father in his red polka-dot pajamas? Aren't those the things you know best? And what about your faith?"

This last, although it was my main point, I added as if it were an afterthought.

Priit's eyes stared mistily off into space. At times their color was like that of a glacial lake, breathtaking but strangely vacant. So full of innocence they seemed, one might wonder whether there was anything there at all.

"It seems to me," I continued, "that one of the cardinal sins a writer can commit is to concoct all sorts of exotic plots and characters when the thing that is most exotic of all is his own life. When people look at you, Priit, they see a life that has had far more than its share of hardship but that daily, mysteriously, triumphs. So why don't you write about that?"

Priit's long, delicate fingers pulled at one end of his moustache. "I have never triumphed over my problems by wallowing in them," he answered hesitantly. "Isn't life painful enough as it is? When I write I want to enjoy myself. For if work isn't a pleasure, why do it? Are you suggesting that all fiction should be autobiographical?"

"No. Only that it should tell the truth. Only that a writer must write with his soul, not just with his imagination."

Already I sensed I had said too much. I had touched a nerve. A wall had gone up between us. What was the point in pursuing this any further? It had never even occurred to me that the strain of writing about his own life might actually be too much for Priit, that perhaps he just wasn't up to it. And when we parted that day he clasped my hand with such warmth, and his eyes were so bright and the crinkles around them so winning, that I felt rebuked, ashamed of myself for having judged his work so harshly. Fine, I thought. Let him go on believing he's turning out great literature. What harm in that? Why rock the boat?

And yet, walking home that day, I found myself pondering whether it was really possible for some things to be too painful to write about. I knew what Priit was saying, yet it struck me as shallow and evasive. Wasn't pain, honestly dealt with, always a tonic rather than a poison? I couldn't understand how a man could be so obviously victorious over his own suffering in real life while apparently shying away from it on paper. Or was it in the very nature of art—for all its claims of probing honesty—to brilliantly palliate pain without ever truly getting at its root? Of all evasions of reality, was art the most sophisticated? Artists, of course, brought this same charge against religion.

All of this I might have forgotten, sweeping it under the carpet, if a few days later Friida hadn't dropped by our house to deliver yet another of Priit's English manuscripts, this time a long novel. "He thinks you'll like this one much better," she said. "It's more true to life. And he said to tell you that he's rewriting several of those stories along the lines you suggested. He really found your comments most helpful."

I was at a loss for words. My fondness for Friida was as great as for Priit. She was a wise and deeply loving woman. Yet now I was seeing a side to her I didn't like—a credulous, foolish side. Was she too deluded about her husband's work? Nothing was more desolating than to be drawn into a web of dishonesty with people one held in high regard. Strangled by white lies (the blackest lies of all), I saw myself walking straight into the trap of being an appreciative reader for writing I despised.

After glancing through the first chapter of the novel I left it sitting on top of the refrigerator for a week. Finally I set aside an evening in which to tackle it, but a hundred pages was almost more than I could endure. The main difference from the stories was that this was a work set in Estonia, and there were some truly wonderful descriptive passages. Indeed, just as before, there was the odd sentence or image so beautiful it nearly broke my heart. But otherwise this novel had the same sprawling, tumid style, the same fantastic cast of characters dreaming, swearing, and hooting their way through life, the same wearisome ebullience, the same noncommittal acceptance of everything under the sun.

"What am I going to do?" I moaned again to my wife.

"Maybe you'll have to level with him."

"You keep changing your advice."

"But you need to do what you think is best."

"Thanks."

If the major problem had been that Priit were deceived about his literary abilities, as indeed the great majority of writers were, then that I could have forgiven. For what was to say that I myself was not so deceived? But what continued to mystify and to madden me, was the religious question. How could such godlessness be excused in a Christian author? Whether they were Christian or not, of course, I tended to have the same problem with most authors of fiction. For I believed in my marrow that literature, in its essence, was inescapably religious. Were not all the oldest and most enduring world classics, from the Bible to the Bhagavad-Gita to Homer, actually works of religious propaganda? There was every reason to believe that their original authors and audiences were far more interested in spiritual values than in literary ones. Yet the modern world had reversed this and seemed to be striving towards a "pure" literature, one that would be entirely free from any religious bias. Literature was trying to disown its own father. The novel itself, the youngest of the genres, was a product of the Enlightenment. It had grown up during the very time in history when God was being systematically blackballed from all science and culture, and therefore it was no wonder if fiction were the most secular and bourgeois of all the arts, godless to the core. Of course a novel or a short story could concern itself with religious themes. But for the author to intrude his own heartfelt beliefs, to treat the existence of God as a simple reality, or seriously to introduce the Lord Himself as a character every bit as alive (and more so) as any of the others—these things were anathema. They showed the height of bad taste. And the case for the direct involvement of Jesus Christ was even more bleak: He was the one obscenity in modern fiction, the one character for whom there could be no "suspension of disbelief." To me the reason for all of this was perfectly obvious: literature was a religion unto itself. And the god of literature was a jealous god indeed.

The more I thought about these things in relation to Priit's writing and the high hopes I had initially held for it, the more I nursed a sense of personal begrudging, even of betrayal. Had I completely misjudged this man? Had my pity for his physical disabilities caused me to overestimate him? Was he, on the inside, nothing but a phony? Perhaps not a true Christian at all? "By their fruit you shall know them," Jesus had warned.

For our next meeting I determined to say nothing at all to Priit about the artistic merits of his novel, nor to offer any flattery, but simply to take him to task on this one issue. I also wondered whether I should urge him to switch to nonfiction, perhaps even to devotional writing, where he might be on safer ground.

This time we met in the coffee shop. I waited while he went through his usual routine of doubling over, gasping for breath, and asking the waitress for a glass of oxygen. It was strange how accustomed one could grow to the sufferings of others. The longer I had known Priit, the more I had taken his disabilities for granted, assuming, I suppose, that he himself did the same. Even his blindness was something I tended to overlook now. One could not stare suffering continually in the eye, and perhaps the central mystery of humanity was its capacity to adapt quite nicely to almost any set of circumstances, no matter how appalling.

Eventually the talk came round to Priit's novel. Before I could say anything, however, he launched into a long explanation of how he had come to write the thing and the problems it had given him. I grew impatient. There were pieces of doughnut smeared on the lip of his coffee cup, and a large crumb had become lodged in one corner of his mouth. The manners of the blind could leave much to be desired, and it was with a peculiar mixture of indifference and alarm that I noticed, as one becomes aware of something in a dream, that my feeling towards Priit in that moment was one of utter revulsion.

"Listen, Priit," I said to him finally. "Before we get down to the details of this novel, I have a bone to pick with you. I have one serious objection that colors the way I read all your work, one fundamental question I cannot get out of my mind. You're a Christian, right? Then tell me, why is your writing not Christian? Why is there nothing in it about God?"

Priit looked truly perplexed. Again there was on his face the expression of a little child caught red-handed, one who either does not know or will not let on that he has done anything wrong.

"Nothing about God?" he asked. "But look, if I had wanted to write about God, I would have been a theologian, not a writer of fiction. I think of my work as being merely to tell stories, plain stories, pure and simple. And isn't every story, finally, about God? It's not as if He can ever really be left out."

"He certainly can be left out," I argued. "He can be deliberately excluded from a man's writing, just as He can be exclud-

ed from a man's life. The whole riddle of faith is that mere
human creatures, dust and ashes, have been given a say as to
how much their own Creator is to be involved in their lives.
Christ invites us to a banquet, but we in turn must invite Him
into every corner of our world and our hearts. If we don't invite Him, He doesn't come."

I went on to give an account of my opinions regarding writing and religion, particularly my view that the great problem
with modern fiction was that God, indeed, had been left out
of it. Priit listened to all of this with his empty green eyes
staring past my shoulder at some indeterminate point, as if
focused on an object only he could see. I began to wonder if
he were listening at all. Had he heard all of this before? The
impossibility of meeting his gaze frustrated me. When I finished there was a long silence between us.

"I don't know what to say," he replied finally. "Except that
as I see it, fiction is nothing but storytelling—a good rip-roar-
ing tale, and that's all. Why should something as innocent as
that need defending? Why complicate it with theology? Is it
necessary, just because I am a Christian, to write the Lord's
name on every page? Is that what makes writing Christian?
Look at the Book of Esther. God is not mentioned in it once,
yet still it is in the Bible. It is a sacred book! And it is full of
the most scandalous goings-on. But even if it is true, as you
seem to imply, that my stories are really not good enough for
the Lord's standards, then what else can I do other than cast
myself at the feet of Jesus, my sweet Savior, and beg His forgiveness? But I cannot write in a way that He has never given
me a desire to write. You are asking the impossible."

Who could find fault with such words? If I had been a
priest and Priit had come to me with this confession, would I
not have absolved him on the spot? Yet even so, I was not
convinced. I felt instinctively that there was still some level at
which he was being evasive, not facing the problem squarely.
Nevertheless, I had had this same conversation before with
Christian writers, ones who were published and well known,

and I knew it led nowhere. What was the point in arguing? Could argument change a man's writing style any more than it could produce faith? I knew Priit was hurt, and suddenly I noticed how impassioned I had grown, furious with the knowledge that I was right. And just then the realization hit home with piercing clarity: one could be right as rain, and still be wrong. What good was it to tell the truth if one did so without love? I was no Alyosha.

As we parted that day it was with the burning awkwardness of having not understood one another, or perhaps with the even darker awareness of having understood too well. For my part I could not help but suspect that what had really come between us was Jesus Himself, and that Priit, for all his sterling qualities, was simply a less committed Christian than myself. A brother, yes, but a "weaker brother." In any case we had arrived at the very impasse that I always seemed to reach with other fiction writers, but that with Priit I had hoped with all my heart to avoid. Was it the Lord, I wondered, or the Evil One, or I myself, who seemed intent on bringing about in every relationship the very conditions that gave rise to strife? Somehow it appeared that all three of us had a hand in it.

Over the next few weeks I saw Priit frequently, and we continued on the most friendly of terms. In fact, precisely because an invisible reserve had sprung up between us, we tended to smile and chat together more warmly than ever. But the subject of writing was not mentioned. One Sunday after church, however, I made a point of talking to Friida about it. As delicately as I could I explained the problem, and then I put it to her directly. "And what about you? What do you think of your husband's work? You must spend hours and hours typing out what he's written!"

Friida bit her lip. Her lined, kindly face at times reminded me exactly of Priit himself. "I'm no judge of literature," she replied cautiously. "But to tell you the truth I do share your concerns. The language, for one thing. The bawdiness. I have no explanation for it. Sometimes I wonder if every man

doesn't have those sorts of thoughts, whether he is a
Christian or not, and Priit simply writes them down. I cannot
say. But you know, in many ways he is like a boy. He plays at
his work. It's all a huge amount of fun. You should see him
when he's hard at it! He talks a blue streak, chattering away in
the voices of his characters, and even hums and sings to himself. Anyone overhearing would think he was mad. And if
he's not enjoying a piece, he simply puts it aside. It has to be
fun or he won't do it. And so, to answer your question, I really think his writing does him tremendous good, just like a
tonic. Whether or not it does anyone else good is another matter. But for him it's a form of therapy, and that is why I have
never dared to bother him about it."

"Therapy?" I said. "You mean, for his illness?"

"Exactly. He's often told me that when he's writing well, he
completely forgets that he's a sick man. The same as when he
plays the piano. The discomfort, all the problems, will actually
go away. And even the blindness. He *sees* the things he's writing about. But there is something else too. When I use this
word therapy it might help you to know that Priit spent several years in a mental hospital. Yes, we have never told you
that. Not that it's any dark secret. But that is how we passed
our first years in Canada. It was a most painful time, much
worse than anything we had gone through in the war. Yet that
is where he met Christ, you see, there in the hospital. I believe it's the only reason he's a sane man today—or alive at all.
So what do I care whether he's a great writer or not? Or
whether his work pleases me? What's important is that his
mind is as clear as a bell, and he's happy, and his heart is the
tenderest heart I have ever known. In his own way I believe
he is a great man. I thank God for him every day."

At home I related to my wife the account of Priit's years in a
mental hospital and his conversion there. "Why doesn't he
write about that?" I said to her excitedly. "What a novel it
would make!"

"Maybe he just isn't up to it."

"Nonsense. How can a man find the strength to overcome such terrible afflictions, both in his flesh and his spirit, yet not have the strength to write about it?"

"Well, maybe he's afraid of giving himself too profoundly to the pursuit of art. You know, with a capital *A*? You're aware yourself of the cost it can exact. And you're forever calling art "the modern idolotry," "the golden calf," and so on. But maybe Priit, underneath it all, is content to be a failure. Didn't you once say you envied him his joyousness? Maybe he needs that light heart just to stay alive."

"Yes, yes, I know what you're saying. But I can't quite buy it. No writer I have ever known was content with failure. And can it really be good "therapy" for a Christian man to create reams and reams of amoral tripe? Surely the best therapy is truth, reality. Does sickness excuse a man from being truthful? It may be, you know, that the Lord is using me to speak to Priit, to challenge him to fulfill his potential. What if he has a truly great book inside him?"

"But have you considered the other possibility?" my wife asked. "That the Lord may be using Priit Laas to speak to you?"

"How do you mean?"

"Just what you've often said yourself: that you cannot understand how great writers can be so wise in their writing, yet so foolish in their living. Will you hold it against Priit if he happens to be the other way around?"

I pondered this. I recalled a Zen koan that posed the question, "He says it, but does he know it?" Yet if Priit really knew it, why then didn't he say it? It did seem to be the case that some authors were themselves greater than the books they wrote, while some were lesser. Perhaps only in the case of the Lord Jesus Christ could it be said that His words were a perfect reflection of who He was.

The conversations with Friida and with my wife kept buzzing in my head, and I kept hearing the sound of Priit's voice as he prayed. And gradually a new mystery took up residence in my mind, like a grain of sand in an oyster. For deep in my heart I had reason to wonder whether Priit Laas, come Judgment Day, might actually be revealed to be a better man than I was, a better Christian. At the same time I was reasonably certain that I was the better writer. But what I didn't know was whether or not I would have wanted the tables turned.

One day in February I walked out into our backyard and heard a new sound in the air. Minutes before I had been sitting at the typewriter, bogged down in my novel and staring glumly out the window. Now, listening intently, I heard the faint but distinct trickle of water beneath the ice in the river, and for just one instant as I stood perfectly still on the bank, it seemed that the entire winter flashed by (and perhaps all of life with it), as if the whole world and particularly myself had been fast asleep in the frozen current and just now was stirring. Day by day after that I watched the river open up, until it no longer seemed such a thrill to see it. People grew anesthetized to the pain of life, but perhaps we were even more inured to its joys.

There was a solid month of rain, during which the river ice seemed not so much to melt as to erode away, forming patterns like those of ancient rock. The rain came first in a thin drizzle, freezing, and then the heavens really opened until one morning I was awakened by what sounded like Niagara Falls right outside our bedroom window. Throwing on boots and raincoat, I rushed out back to see that the river had risen by several feet and was clogged with broken ice floes. Somewhere upstream the pack must have ruptured, and now the remaining ice was all being ripped out in one great headlong whoosh. With deafening, spellbinding violence the glut kept up for nearly an hour, until finally in a series of tired sighs the river subsided and returned to normal.

And suddenly it was spring. That same day the cloud cover thinned and the sun broke through gloriously. But in the evening when we went in high spirits to the Laases' for Bible study, it was only to find that Priit had fallen ill. He was confined to bed and we carried on without him but gathered later in his room for prayer.

The following afternoon I stopped by to see him. Friida showed me in, and right away I realized that he wasn't up to having visitors. Even overnight there had been an alarming deterioration. He was flat on his back, with his mouth wide open, and his body under the covers seemed barely to be there. His white hair shone like a corona, but in his eyes was a new, an alien, brightness. Suddenly, uncharacteristically, I was overcome with tears.

Later that week Priit was admitted to the local hospital, and a day after that he was transferred to the district hospital a hundred miles down the valley. He had developed an ulcerous sore on one of his legs. The infection spread, exacerbated by diabetes, and for three weeks he lay in a fever. Friida went down and stayed with her sister in order to be near him, but the Bible-study group continued, meeting in a different home, and we prayed for the Laases. Meanwhile the days grew longer and there was more and more sunshine, and the birds came back and spring like green blood filled the valley.

Eventually we learned that Priit's leg was to be amputated. By that point, however, the gangrene had so weakened him that there was significant doubt as to whether he could survive an operation. The night before the surgery we called Friida and prayed with her over the telephone. She sounded calm, even cheerful. "Priit is fine," she reported. "The fever has been bad, but in his clear moments he's been perfectly at peace. The worse things look, the more he praises God."

Then she told us an ironic piece of news: that very day word had come that Priit was to have a book published, his first ever. Even at that point, I'm afraid, my own initial reaction to the news was not a charitable one. Yet as it turned out it was not any of his fiction that had been accepted, but a translation of poetry he had done years before. The work was an obscure Estonian epic from the nineteenth century, and the project was being funded by the Estonian cultural organization. Still, it seemed a miracle, and a most unlikely one. For what if Priit were to die on the operating table the next morning? If God wanted to intervene supernaturally, I thought, why didn't He do it by saving Priit's leg, or his life? What good would a published book do him now?

That night I found myself taking a good long look at my own two legs, at their strange numinous flesh, and at the flesh of my face in the mirror and the lambent jelly of my two uncertain eyes. And I thought about the slow process of amputation that death performs all through our bodies and on all the work of our hands. I thought about the evanescence of writing. "Of making many books there is no end," wrote Ecclesiastes, who had written a book himself. I liked to think that I was ready to die, even eager about going to Heaven and being with Christ. Yet at that moment, to my surprise, it felt as though I had never really thought about any of these things at all.

Friida called us the next day to relate the news that Priit had survived his operation. Not only that, he was sitting up and "yakking away." She said it wasn't likely he would ever walk again, but, as he himself observed, he'd gotten "good mileage out of that drumstick." Apparently as a young man he had walked everywhere, often hiking six or eight miles to see a friend rather than driving the car. One of his favorite comments about Estonia was that the automobile, thank heaven, was still too expensive for the average Joe to own. "He figures he did more walking in a year," reported Friida, "than most folks do in an entire lifetime "

A week later our Bible-study group received a note from Priit in his own handwriting: "No more leg," it read, "but still in one piece. Many thanks for all your prayers. The Lord has been good. He gives, He takes away, blessed be His name. He can have the rest of me any time He likes."

As I lay in bed that night with my wife I lamented, "Why couldn't he write that way in his books?" And then I answered my own question. "What he's got—you could never capture it in a story, could you? Fiction was made for showing sin, not righteousness."

Priit remained in the hospital throughout that Spring. He was on physiotherapy, but there were further complications. And eventually it came time for us to return to the city. On our last Sunday in the valley it happened that the Lutheran minister had just returned from his holidays, and I sat with my wife in the little white church and listened to the only memorable sermon we had heard all that year, on the text of Psalm 147:18: "The Lord sends His word to thaw the ice; He stirs up His breezes and the waters flow."

That night it turned cool and we built our last fire in the wood stove, and when it was nice and hot I threw into it the whole manuscript of the novel I'd been working on that year, chapter by chapter. I wasn't trying to be melodramatic. But the thing had given me nothing but frustration, and I wanted to be rid of it and make a clean start. There was something rejuvenating just in watching the manuscript pages curl up in the flames. I was more pensive than sad. And I found myself wondering, as I sat before the ancient dancing firelight, whether I might really have learned something that year: that the greatest literature is not what is written, but what is lived.

Fictional Love

Meanwhile, there are three things that endure: faith, hope, and love.
But the greatest of these is love.

—1 CORINTHIANS 13:13

If Paul had been a Christian novelist rather than a great apostle, he might have written the following: "There are three things that endure: setting, plot, and character. But the greatest of these is character."

However much avant garde fiction writers may have tried to do away with them, the traditional fundamentals of setting, plot, and character have always been and will remain the three elements essential to all storytelling. Thus, "A certain man [character] went down from Jerusalem to Jerico [setting] and fell among thieves [plot]." Jesus really knew how to pack a sentence!

Although Paul, in the famous thirteenth chapter of 1 Corinthians, was talking about the art of life rather than the art of fiction, his point was precisely the same. Faith, hope, and love, he concluded, are the central concerns of Christianity. Without these we have nothing, just as we cannot tell a true story without building the foundation upon setting, plot, and character. In either case to lose touch with the three basics is to lose touch with reality itself.

Indeed between these two threesomes there can even be traced something of a one-to-one correspondence. For to the individual Christian caught in the strange no-man's-land between spirit and flesh, *faith* might be termed the *setting*, the place where one must take a stand between heaven and earth in order to work out the story of one's salvation. And as for *hope*, is that not a kind of *plot*, impelling the believer onwards toward a conclusion at once astonishing and inevitable?

Then there is *love*. And just as Paul goes on to say "the great-est of these is love," so the Christian storyteller must confess that the most important dimension of his art is that of *character*. Character is the backbone of fiction, for, as we have already said, the real purpose of fiction is the exploration and revelation of human nature. As Paul states in the previous verse of this same passage, one day "we shall see face to face . . . we shall know fully, even as we are fully known" (1 Cor. 13:12). Exactly this, in earthly terms, is the aim of fiction, this same encounter-in-depth with the mysteries of the heart. To define this more precisely, the fundamental goal of fiction is to bring a living character (the reader) into a real face-to-face *relationship* with a fictional character in such a way that the heart of the former may be revealed and transformed.

This is the secret of fiction's power. And need it be added that this is a power that generally is exploited and used destruc-tively? Even in the Bible there are examples of the godless mis-use of fiction, such as the story of the seven brothers in Mark 12, which the Sadducees relate to Jesus in an effort to trap Him into denying the truth of the Resurrection. The story itself is a fascinating one, but its whole motive is to confuse Jesus by arousing His sympathies for a hopelessly tangled human dilem-ma, and it must be admitted that this identical motive underlies much of the world's great literature. Only when the art of fic-tion is practised under the guiding influence of genuine love can the powerful mystical encounter between reader and char-acter be a truly creative and healthy one. Otherwise it is a thing that smacks of black magic and the demonic. It is voodoo and shamanism in the guise of literature.

Consider the power behind the concluding line of the parable of the good Samaritan: "Go and do likewise" (Luke 10:37). Nothing could be more obvious than that Jesus intended the character of this fictional Samaritan to make its way into the living soul of the young law expert standing before Him, in such a way as to radically change the man. It was a kind of mystical blood transfusion that Jesus was after, a loving miracle of transformation, every bit as intentional as when He stuck His fingers into the ears of a deaf man.

But the Devil also seeks to transform people, and in his hands too fiction is a wonder drug, a powerful alchemy.

Again, consider the concluding remark that follows a session of the Lord's storytelling in Matthew 21:45: "When the chief priests and the Pharisees heard Jesus' parables, they knew He was talking about *them*." Right here is the essential trick of fiction: it is the drawing, lulling, or otherwise enticing of the real audience into a direct identification with the fictional characters. As soon as such identification has taken place (whether for good or for evil), then the story has done its work. Then the *spell* of the fiction is complete, because at that point what was unreal (or what was real only in the author's imagination) suddenly merges with or spills over into objective reality.

Thus the rigid boundary that the world likes to pretend exists between *fact* and *fiction* is, biblically speaking, a somewhat misleading one. Fictional stories are meant to cast a spell, to act as a kind of prayer (or curse), and thus to be woven seamlessly into real life. Their power derives not so much from their artistry as from the character of the author and the purity of his or her motives. This curious fact becomes crystal clear in the parables of Jesus. True, from a purely artistic standpoint they are masterpieces. But their real power stems not from art, but from who it is who is doing the telling and from the fact that, as in the case of Scheherazade in *The Arabian Nights*, with every word the very life of the storyteller is on the line.

Similarly, in a famous scene in 2 Samuel 12, the prophet Nathan risks his own life when he comes to King David and, by means of a parable, denounces his sinful conduct with Uriah and Bathsheba. The story Nathan tells the king is not a true one (although the prophet initially leads him to think it is), yet when David discovers that his own behavior has been exactly parallel to that of the parable's cruel protagonist, he is cut to the heart. Mere fiction slices him open like a sword. For while the fictional character is not real, the relationship Nathan succeeds in choreographing between this character and King David *is a real relationship*. And ultimately the potion of this imaginary being proves stronger than that of the king's love for a real, living woman.

In "Priit Laas" what happens is that the narrator's abstract theological theories (which concern, interestingly enough, the topic of Christian fiction) are shattered as he is brought into a living relationship with a "real" person. He experiences the truth of 1 Corinthians 13, that "the greatest of these is love," and that without love, the best and soundest theology in the world is rendered meaningless. The story's governing motif, perhaps, comes not so much in the final sentence as it does in the narrator's insight that "You can be right as rain, but if it is without love you are wrong." And just as this devastating truth pierces the storyteller, so should it also (providing the author has done a good job) in some way pierce the reader, as he too meets, gets to know, and hopefully comes to love this fictional character, Priit Laas.

And now I must blurt out a personal confession. When I set out to write this story, I planned it as a vehicle for expressing some of my own ideas about Christian fiction (ideas that, as should be clear throughout this book, I still hold to firmly). Accordingly I modeled the narrator, more or less, on myself, while the title character I invented to serve as a foil for my pet theories. This sort of blatantly propagandistic set-up, by the way, is considered by fiction writers to be the unforgiveable sin, the kiss of death for serious literature. Nevertheless I went ahead and did it shamelessly.

But a funny thing happened to me on the way to the type-writer each day: I began to feel myself drawn into a real relationship with my fictional character. This is a phenomenon that all novelists know about. The invented character comes to life, as it were, walks right into the author's study and starts peering over his shoulder and offering critical suggestions. And under the hand of an imaginary being the author himself begins to change.

This had happened to me before as a writer, but never so powerfully as in the case of Priit Laas. Naturally I resisted the operation, fought it tooth and nail, because, of course, I did not really love Priit Laas. I wanted to use him, not love him. I had my own plans about how the story should end and how my own ideas (not only about fiction, but about what it means to be a true believer) would be vindicated over those of my character. Yet day after day it was a three-dimensional Priit who took his blue pencil to this carefully constructed outline, and though I struggled and struggled against him, he for his part was quietly determined to wrest control from the arrogant author and to move the plot in his own direction. This went on for months, in draft after draft. I just couldn't make the thing come out the way I wanted it to. The conflict was all rather subtle, of course, and at the time I had no real idea of what was going on. But in the end I threw in the towel, symbolically burned my manuscript, and rewrote the whole story in such a way as to let this old, one-legged, blind Estonian have the final word and emerge (in the deepest sense) victorious.

And I came to this simply because in the final analysis there are only three things that matter in life, and art is not among them, and neither is ideology. Rather, the three are faith, hope, and love. That's all there is to it. And the greatest of these is love.

Yet still, how I wish that Priit Laas could have seen my point too and forsaken his godless writing! When I meet up with him in Heaven I'm almost sure we'll agree.

Bound for Glory

It was Christmas Eve. A light rain was falling as I set off across the platform. The weight of my bag felt good, and I had that feeling of self-importance that sometimes comes when embarking on a journey alone. I was certain no one on the train would know me, and dressed as I was in my best suit and a brand new trench coat, I would very likely be taken for a person of some distinction. A man of mystery, even to myself.

It was close to midnight and the station was unusually busy, though not with the hustle and bustle of a daylight rush hour but with the eerie trance-like commotion of darkness. Everywhere hunched bodies, shadowy but also shiny with the black gloss of the rain, seemed to scud along like ghostly sail-boats, gliding as in a dream. All the lights on the platform bloomed with haloes of mist, softly rainbow tinted, and the pavement was black and slick like a sheet of ice in moonlight. As I fell in with the movement of the throng I saw another man, one even more mysterious than I, walking directly be-neath me, at each step planting the soles of his feet against mine, his head thrust far away into the dark glimmering sky of another world.

The train waited, warm and steaming and spirited like a high-mettled horse. I found my car, mounted the steps, and upon opening the door I felt a soft rush of wind. The lights and warmth from inside were most inviting, and I looked forward to finding a seat by myself and relaxing. But a sur-prise awaited me, for not only were there no empty seats but the passengers were jammed in so tightly that the seats themselves were obscured, and even many of the windows were entirely hidden behind precarious piles of coats and luggage. People held large boxes and baskets on their laps. Trunks and bedrolls and canvas packs filled the overhead racks and plugged even the center aisle and the spaces between the seats. Never before had I seen a train car so crowded.

Quickly I turned to go. But while crossing over the coupling into the next car I met a porter who told me abruptly, "There's no use looking for another spot, sir. The whole train's like this." Upon questioning him further I learned of an astonishing announcement by the authorities, to the effect that all the country's borders were to be thrown open to emigration for Christmas Day. No one knew why, nor exactly what was happening, but thousands of people had packed up all they could carry and were rushing toward the border. It was an unprecedented event, and the whole country was astir with it. For my part, having spent all that day and evening poring over my research in the state library, naturally I'd had no news. And in any case, since I was a foreigner, this was not something that touched me directly.

After glancing into the next car and finding it no less crowded, I turned back to the first car and sat down on my suitcase, with knees to chest and my back against one of the metal seat braces. There were so many passengers that it was impossible to sit anywhere without being scrunched up against another body. I felt slightly panicky, claustrophobic, but decided to make the best of things, and slowly it dawned on me what an extraordinary event I had been caught up in. A Ph.D. candidate in history, I experienced the ambiguous thrill of suddenly finding myself a participant in the living drama of history in the making. What great political upheaval had taken place? I wondered. In my own country the reports of it were no doubt being broadcast, right this moment, on special news bulletins.

Glancing around at this trainload of human souls packed tight as sardines, I was reminded, involuntarily, of the Jews in World War II being shipped off in boxcars to concentration camps. Yet apparently in this case these people were traveling towards freedom. They were people who, burdened as they were, had left practically everything behind them, and who were prepared to travel through the darkness of Christmas Eve into a totally unknown future, with the sole hope of gaining their freedom. I began to feel an admiration for them and an interest in who they were.

Bunched up against me was a bearded young man in a striped overcoat, and directly above me, so that I sat at her feet, was a girl dressed in a sky-blue cape that came right to the floor. With dark radiant hair and almond eyes that gazed wonderingly out from the blue loop of her hood, she looked hardly old enough to be a mother, and yet in her lap she cradled a tiny baby who was almost invisible inside a bundle of blankets. This was the only infant on the train, though there were about a dozen older children present, all sitting on laps or tucked away in the narrowest of corners. The other passengers were men and women in their thirties and forties, most wearing the drab, bulky clothing of the lower classes. There were men with bushy moustaches and heavy women with kerchiefs encircling round, oily faces. Their features were plain, yet etched with a peculiar determination. They were faces not used to much laughter, faces made, it occurred to me, especially for the bearing of hardship and pain.

All of us were anxious for the train to start moving. But it didn't budge. It was now well past midnight, yet no one slept, not even the children. They squirmed and chattered, and the adults too engaged in animated conversation. Actual waves of excitement ran through the car, like wind over a wheat field. It was as though these people were one single body, charged with the same blood. There were periodic shouts of "The best Christmas present ever!" and "Let's get this thing rolling!" Even the silent heaps of baggage bespoke movement and anticipation. But the train didn't budge. The night was very dark outside; black beads of rain bled against the gray windows.

From where I sat I glimpsed a few strings of Christmas lights winking hazily in the distance.

Chatting to the man beside me, I learned that he was from the country and had already traveled several hundred kilometers that evening. He had left everything, he said—friends, family, a good job, many possessions. But he had no regrets. "This is the very thing we have been waiting for all our lives," he said. He had a close-cropped beard and spoke quietly and seriously. He had the rough hands of a worker, and his face, though young, was deeply lined, with a quality of such gentleness to it that it gave me an awkward feeling just to look at him. Glancing up at the girl with the baby, I asked him if she were his wife. No, he answered, they were only engaged, and this surprised me. Unwed pregnancies were still a thing of scandal in that country, and besides, this man struck me for some reason more as a husband than as a boyfriend or fiancé. He had an air of responsibility about him, and though shy he seemed not at all ashamed over the baby and spoke quite candidly of wedding plans.

Still the train had not moved. One o'clock came, then two o'clock, and the mood of buoyant expectancy gave way gradually to one of agitation. "Something must have gone wrong," was the gist of the talk. Either something was mechanically wrong with the train, or else, more serious, we had run into some bureaucratic snag. As time wore on it was the latter eventuality that seemed more and more the likely one. No railroad officials were to be found. It was a fair trek back to the station house, and none of us wanted to get off to enquire, for fear the train might leave without us. Knowing well the ways of the authorities and the capriciousness of the system we were caught in, we all knew there was nothing to do but stay put and wait it out patiently. The boisterous cries of "Let's get this machine out of here!" died away. The group of people towards the back, who had struck up a chorus of Christmas carols, stopped singing. The night grew colder and blankets were brought out. The rain had turned freezing, and all the windows were hung with black curtains of ice. Fear grew in the car like crystallized fingers of frost. There was every reason to suppose that the government might change its mind, or that this entire affair would turn out to be some cruel hoax.

Towards three o'clock the door of the compartment finally opened, and a tall man stepped in. He wore a gray floor-length cape covered with sparkling beads of ice, and in concealed arms he cradled an automatic rifle. From his officer's cap, with its crest of gold wings, I recognized him as a state soldier. He stood squarely in the open doorway in a position to command the whole car, and I saw that two other soldiers, also with rifles, were directly behind him. They were all tall men, each larger than any of the passengers, and their bell-shaped, ice-spangled ponchos made them appear even more enormous.

When the first officer spoke, we were all surprised at how quiet his voice was. He had a thick dialect that I found hard to understand, but his message was very clear from the actions that followed. He began to walk through the car, poking the barrel of his weapon straight into the chests of each of the children, one by one. Softly he would enquire who the parents were, then swing the rifle in their direction, and with gentle insistence instruct the child to go and stand by the back door where two more soldiers stood guard. These two, along with the pair at the front, held their rifles level at their shoulders and swept them slowly back and forth over all the passengers, while the first man passed methodically and inexorably through the car. It was a very quiet process. Everyone was terrified. No one uttered a word of protest, and each child was unhesitatingly obedient. There was no crying. Their small faces were firmly set, darkly brave, each as serious as any adult's. They looked like little soldiers themselves.

Not until the officer reached my own aisle did I suddenly recall the baby. How would the young mother ever bring herself to surrender him? I wondered. Briefly I entertained a wild fantasy of saving the infant myself, somehow using the leverage of my foreign citizenship to protect him or perhaps even putting up a struggle. But then I thought of the four automatic weapons that were trained upon us and realized how dangerous it would be to make any move whatsoever, especially as we did not yet have any clear idea what the soldiers' intention was. The commander spoke so quietly and was so strangely gentle in his actions. Perhaps there was simply such a crush of people heading for the borders that they had somehow to be separated and sent on in stages. Such a possibility seemed wildly unlikely, but we all held our breath and hoped against hope.

Miraculously the baby was missed, passed over, and the grim operation of selection continued on into the back of the car. As I glanced up at the young mother, a chill passed through me when I realized that she had concealed the infant under her blue cape. There was the slightest bulge at her stomach, as if she were just beginning to show signs of pregnancy. Her face was serene but very pale. I looked quickly away.

One by one a dozen frail and silent children were gathered at the back of the train. The head soldier had threaded his way down the whole length of the car, over bodies and piles of baggage, just like some terrible harvester picking off the tenderest shoots. Finally he stood at the back, in the very midst of the children, and issued a curt statement, his voice so hushed now that it was difficult to hear him at all. From what I could make out, he told us we were all traitors to the state and deserved to be shot on the spot. But instead only the children were to be sacrificed, and the rest of us would be allowed to proceed on that basis. If it was freedom we wanted, then freedom we would get. It was our own choice. And with that he turned and disappeared, herding the children out through the open door so swiftly and efficiently that not one thing could have been done to stop him. There were sudden cries of alarm, screams. Cold terror gripped everyone. Even I shuddered to think what the parents must be feeling. A couple of the men jumped to their feet as if to do something, but the two rifles at the front swung round towards them, and the men froze. There was weeping. At any moment we half expected to hear shots from outside the train, but none came. Finally all the soldiers left, from both front and back, and stood on the coupling platforms just outside the doors. And as the full awareness of what had just happened flooded in, an enormous anguish seized our hearts, settling down like the whole weight of the dark icy sky caving in on us this Christmas night.

Only minutes later our car started to roll, at first gently, almost imperceptibly, and then with great creaks and groans of the steel couplings and wheels. Shudders rang like shots down the whole length of the train. We picked up speed, and soon we were separated from those dozen children as completely as if they were on the other side of the world. We could only guess at what their fate might be. The soldier had spoken of "sacrifice." Would they be killed on the spot, then? Or was it that the state wished to retain its children? All we knew was that the opening of the borders appeared now to be some diabolical scheme, perhaps intended to single out all those citizens who were secretly disloyal to the state, and with one terrible blow both to punish and to eliminate them.

And so we rolled on through the night, the soft clacking of the wheels like the sound of the pins and bars of fate falling into place around us. There was scant talk now. Heads hung down, and bodies were motionless, stunned with remorse. A few women wept silently. It was indeed a time of painful reflection for each one of us, as all shared to some extent in the impossible burden of the parents' grief. Over and over in their minds they would be reviewing how things might have been different, wishing of course that they had stayed at home, reproaching themselves bitterly for having given in to such foolish dreams of liberty. Compelled now to emigrate and condemned to live with the loss of their children, they would carry forever the wound of their own ill-fated decision.

I did notice a few, though, among those who were not parents, whose mood seemed mostly one of relief. "At least now," I heard one woman remark, "they ought to let the rest of us go in peace. Surely the sacrifice of all those young and innocent lives will be enough to buy freedom for the rest of us." And I must confess I had mixed feelings myself. Naturally I had been impatient about the delay. I was looking forward to spending the holidays with my girlfriend and her family. Even as a student of history I had no desire for history itself to interrupt and alter my personal plans. And yet I could not escape the sense of my lot being thrown in with these other passengers. It was something that happened on a journey, unavoidably, even in the most ordinary of circumstances. We became one with our fellow travelers, no matter who they were. We discovered, as if it were something brand new to us, what it meant to share with strangers. And on this night especially, with its tragic turn of events, I could hardly help but be filled with an unusual compassion for those around me. Whatever else might happen I knew that a deep scar would be left in all of our memories for every Christmas hereafter. I thought again of the young man and woman nearest to me and of their tiny baby. Would they be able to smuggle him across the border? The man, I noticed, had reached up and was holding the girl's hand. Their heads were bowed, and there was the slightest quivering of their lips. I realized that they must be praying.

It was over an hour before we came to the next station. There was loud screeching of steel as the train ground to a halt. We were all startled when the compartment door opened and the same tall soldier entered and stood there in the doorway once again, his wet rain cape like a great, dazzling pair of wings folded about his body. A single cold shudder ran through all of us. Hate rose into the air like an incense. This time the dreaded officer did not make his way through the car but simply announced that all the male passengers were to get up in an orderly fashion and leave by the back door. There was a stunned silence, and for a moment no one moved. But these were people who had long been used to taking orders from the authorities. And now, as before, there were two pairs of rifles trained directly upon them. So after a moment of embracing, kissing, and squeezing hands, in surprisingly quick order the car was completely emptied of all its men.

All, that is, except for myself. For as the last of the men were filing out and being met by soldiers at the rear, I rose to my feet, trembling, and begged a word with the man in charge. Of course I was terrified he would mow me down, no questions asked. But hurriedly I explained that I was a foreign citizen and waved my passport and papers in the air for him to inspect. He made his way toward me, leafed through the documents, and appeared satisfied that they were in order. Without a word, then, he turned away and he and the other soldiers departed, their great capes swishing like the rain itself. The train started up without delay, and soon we were buried again in motion and in night.

The car seemed monstrously empty now, as empty as if a thousand people had left. The raw sense of shock was, if possible, even greater than it had been before. As far as I could tell there had not been a single unattached woman in the car. Every one of them had been separated from a husband, children, or both. Things could not possibly have turned out any worse. It seemed clear now that there would be no emigration at all. What appeared to be happening was that men, women, and children were being split up, perhaps to be shipped off to separate camps. It occurred to me that I might soon have the train all to myself—a strange irony as I recalled my initial disappointment upon seeing the crowded seats. For by this point I would gladly have ridden on top of the baggage rack if only that car could have been filled once again and all of us pass safely over the border together. But it was not to be, and a lump of guilt clotted in my breast as I pondered my sterile immunity to the evil that was rampant all around. My good suit of clothes, my new coat, my Ph.D. thesis, and my citizenship papers all appeared suddenly detestable, standing as they did like rolls of barbed wire between me and these poor persecuted folk. Was there no way at all that I could help them, nor even express solidarity with their plight? Nothing in the world so demanded to be shared as suffering. (Yet how little did I realize that this idealistic wish of mine was soon to be granted!)

All the women now were silent, save one who prattled incessantly in a strident, nerve-wracking voice that put us all more on edge than ever. As there was no longer any shortage of seats, I moved up and took the spot next to the girl in blue. I kept thinking what a horrible situation all these women were in, and yet how much worse it would be for a woman with a child. So far the little one had not made a sound the whole night. Through an opening in the blue cape I could just see his face, tiny as a fist, pink as apple petals, calm and radiant as a sunrise. I think I did feel more peaceful myself just being beside him, having him to look at. It struck me that children were really far better at comforting adults than the other way around.

It was sometime after five o'clock when the train began to slow down once again. I could see nothing outside. Not a single light glimmered in all the countryside. We appeared to be in the middle of nowhere. When the train came to a full stop there was no sound but the distant hum of its engine and the dry rattle of splinters of freezing rain against the windows. In spite of the whole grim weight of our foreboding, it still came as a surprise when once again the tall soldier appeared at the front of the car, his cape white and shining with its veneer of ice, and it was a surprise too when he said, in a voice more hushed than the night itself, that this was where the women must get off. Yet this time there was no hesitation, there being no one left now for the women to be separated from. As one body they rose from their seats and moved like a company of ghosts down the aisle toward the exit. And as they did so I felt something that at first was like the hand of death itself brushing against me, like freezing rain spattering all over my body. For the girl in the blue cape, even as she rose to go, quickly and stealthily as a thief had slipped her baby into my lap. She put him right against my stomach and deftly covered him with the open flap of my coat. And then she was gone.

I went rigid with alarm. My stomach twisted instantly into a hard fist of rejection. I wanted to jump up, to cry out, to make some desperate gesture, but my arms and legs felt shackled to the seat. I wished now that I too could have left the train, but I was paralyzed. And even if I had been capable of moving or making a sign, I dared not. Everything happened so quickly that there was no time to think, no time for anything but to watch helplessly as the beautiful girl in the long blue cape passed between the soldiers at the rear of the car and disappeared like a vision into the black, raining night.

And suddenly I was all alone. More alone, it seemed, than I had ever been in my life. Alone except for a strange tiny bundle of breathing pink flesh that I concealed involuntarily under my coat. The train started to move, and panic swept through me like fire. I felt sick, as if I might actually vomit. I thought of running to the exit and heaving the infant out into the ditch. Anything to get rid of it. Who would know? The soldiers were now gone from the platform. The drama of this Christmas night, for me, ought to have been all over now, but instead things had taken an unimaginable twist.

Still I sat motionless. I dared not even look at the baby. What in the world had possessed the mother to do such a thing? Perhaps she had never wanted a child in the first place? After all, she wasn't even married. But no, hadn't she already gone to extraordinary lengths to protect the baby? Suddenly I guessed at the truth: that this mother was desperate for her child to stay alive, at any cost, and get safely across the border into freedom—so desperate, in fact, that she was willing even to be separated from him herself! Knowing that the soldiers would eventually discover her secret and take him from her anyway, she had opted for the only other course open to her. Furthermore I surmised that she probably had been planning this move ever since the time of the last fateful stop. How excruciatingly painful it must have been for her to contemplate it. Could it be that she had detected something in me, perhaps in the way I looked at the baby, that caused her to trust me? Yet God knows I had not looked upon him with any real love, but more with that grotesque mask of trumped-up innocence adults learn to put on automatically for children. I felt mysteriously that if anyone at all had loved and could be trusted, it was not I, but he, this tiny hidden one.

As there was no need now to leave him concealed, I finally took the child out from under my coat to have a good look at him. He was still fast asleep. He wore a light blue knitted bonnet, and his face shone out from it like a rosy patch of dawn sky. Perhaps there was nothing in the world so beautiful as the sleeping face of a baby. It presented such a contrast with the night's evil, with the vast web of peril and tragedy in which I myself had suddenly become implicated. I recalled the parents, during the last hour they had been together, clasping hands and praying. I was not one to pray myself, but now all at once I did find that my lips began to move in the stillness. The words came haltingly, uneasily, and I suppose they were addressed more to the little baby than to anyone else (as a man will converse even with an animal for reassurance), yet as I spoke them I did enjoy a few moments of great peace, great comfort. The sick feeling subsided, and I noticed how astonishingly light the child was. I was just beginning to feel his warmth. The long journey with its tense succession of events fell away into unreality as the baby glowed in my arms like one bright candle lit in the night, which makes a complete world of all it illumines while turning everything else to darkness.

Right then, I suppose, I tried to resolve to do everything in my power to defend the child, whatever the cost might be. Yet even as this proposition presented itself I saw my courage fail-ing. Wouldn't it be better for all concerned just to leave him behind in his own native country? What if he should start crying at the crucial moment of passing through customs? Or what if I should be searched? The one thing that had kept me from feeling any personal sense of danger this night—my passport—suddenly seemed the flimsiest detail in the world in which to place any confidence, a mere worthless scrap of pa-per. What good was that in a country where families were being wrenched apart and the whole political balance had caved in overnight? The longer I gazed down at this helpless bit of life in my lap, the more acutely was I aware of my own vulnerability, my own utter helplessness. For I saw that the great world held onto me even more precariously than I held onto this infant, and with even less willingness, and still less love. Had anyone ever looked down on me, I wondered, and debated whether to hand me over to the authorities, toss me into a ditch, or else risk their own life to save me?

From then on my plight worsened steadily. It was the hour before dawn and I had had no sleep. My mind played tricks and my nerves quivered with fear and exhaustion. I was in-tensely lonely, and the heaps of baggage in the car evoked a weird impression of the ghostly presence of all the departed passengers. I tried to form some plan of action for getting through customs, but I could not keep my thoughts steady. Moreover, just as I had feared, the baby woke up now and began to cry. I had no idea what to do or how to comfort him. I was no mother, and no longer was he a beautiful, sleeping abstraction, the ideal of innocence, but rather a live, kicking person, making demands. I had wanted a nice quiet trip, not this. But he wailed and wailed, as if to wake the dead, almost as if he sensed, even more acutely than I, all that lay ahead.

My panic increased as clusters of lights and then lighted buildings and streets began to appear in the windows, and I realized we must already be entering the border city. The train slowed, and for the longest time it crawled at an agonizing pace, clacking ominously like something being bumped along over stone. I knew we would soon be at the central station, and desperately I tried everything I could think of to silence the baby's crying. I tried to will myself into composure, hoping that that in itself might comfort him. It even occurred to me that, if worst came to worst, I might knock him unconscious. That is how totally resolved I was, by this point, that he should not fall into the hands of the authorities. But finally, as the station house came in sight, I simply prayed with all my heart that something would silence this confounded baby.

The train stopped. We were under the dark dome of the station. I tucked the child under my coat and did up the buttons. The darkness in there did seem to quiet him some. I could pretend I had a bad cough, I decided, to muffle the sound more. I planned to leave my suitcase behind, as it would be too awkward to carry. I was just trying to calm myself and to go over things once more in my mind when the door of the compartment opened and in walked the tall state soldier, bigger than any man I had ever seen. He came straight up to me and stood there, towering. I thanked God that the baby was now perfectly quiet. At the same time I knew that I could not possibly get out of my seat with the man standing right there. I might as well have been nailed down. "It's time now, sir," said the soldier in English. "I'll have to ask you to come with me."

Though his accent was perfect I thought perhaps I had misunderstood him. I stared.

Then he added, "You're under arrest, sir. You cannot go any further. You'll have to leave the train now."

"But you can't," I protested, almost under my breath. "You can't . . . can't take me. Not *me*!" I could barely find my voice. "I'm a citizen of . . ." I would have reached for my papers then, but they were inside my buttoned coat.

Once again there were other soldiers standing at the back of the car, rifles at the ready. The commander angled his head meaningfully towards them and then looked back at me.

"I'm under orders, sir," he said. "I think you'd better come."

Motioning me to follow, he walked away down the aisle. I experienced a moment of total confusion and dismay. This was not at all something I had anticipated. What was I to do?

I rose slowly to my feet. And as I did so I let the baby slide down gently between my legs, still inside the coat, all the way to the floor. I pretended to be gathering luggage together, checking things over.

"You won't be needing your baggage, sir," said the soldier from the end of the aisle.

Glancing once, quickly, at the floor, I saw the little bundle of blankets there, almost hidden under the seat. He was so good and quiet: I really loved him then. This was our only chance. The train might still be searched and unloaded, but it might also pass through unchecked. At least there remained one slim hope that someone other than a soldier might discover him. Like his own mother, then, I thought it better to leave him to Providence than to see him fall into the hands of the authorities. At least, that is what I told myself. But was the truth, perhaps, that I simply abandoned him?

In any case I left, following the soldiers out into the early dawn. It was still dark on the platform, but at the end of the long tunnel that arched over the tracks there was a glimmering patch of eggshell-white sky. We walked towards it. It was Christmas morning, I remembered. It felt good to stretch my legs. The air was cool and fresh. My responsibility was over, I felt, and a great weight had passed from my shoulders. I had not a care in the world for my own safety.

The soldiers, three of them, escorted me into the station house, took me down a long hallway with beautiful old marble arches and then underneath a gigantic dome and on into another hallway. Our footsteps rang out like gavels. I felt an absurd sense of importance at being given such special treatment. Finally we arrived at a plain wooden doorway and I was shown into a small room, all white, high-ceilinged, with noth-

ing in it but a desk and chair. Two of the soldiers took up
positions at the door while the man in charge seated himself
at the desk and gestured for me to stand before him. He had
removed his hat and rain cape and was dressed in an ordinary
blue suit much like my own. I was surprised to see that he
was not wearing the state military uniform.

He began by informing me that I had been found guilty of a
great number of crimes. He had a thick sheaf of papers in
front of him, which I soon gathered to be a dossier on me. As
he listed the charges I grew more and more astounded. They
were things that concerned not only my movements in this
country but activities at home as well. In fact, there were
things that went right back to my childhood. Who could this
man be who seemed to know everything there was to know
about me, even the things that were most unutterable? I was
so bewildered that I fell into a sort of trance while his deep
voice droned on and on and my whole life was paraded before
me. Wrongs and hurts that I had completely forgotten or suppressed became suddenly as vivid as if they were happening
that very moment, and it seemed that not a single transgres-
sion, not so much as a ghost of a thought, had been over-
looked. Everything had been meticulously recorded, and all of
it was now laid matter-of-factly, officially, before me, almost as
if it were information pertaining to someone else. For strangely, throughout this process, I felt no sense of guilt or condem-
nation but only a numbed and amazed relief at having all
these shameful secrets finally exposed, spoken aloud by one
who did not flinch before their horror.

When I emerged from this reverie (how long it took I have
no idea; it seemed to happen in the twinkling of an eye) I
looked in front of me and all I could see was a wall of fire.
The desk and its great sheaf of papers were consumed in a
blaze of flames so hot and suffocating that I had to shield my
face and turn away. And there at the door was the tall soldier,
beckoning me. I saw that he had donned his rain cape once
again, but now it was a brilliant white, like a robe made of

light itself, and his rifle had become a sword that he carried upright in front of him. I followed him down still another long hallway that eventually brought us outside into a dazzling new morning where the sun shone with a brightness that was like the sound of thousands of crashing cymbals in the sparkling air. The freezing rain from the previous night had left a glistening patina of ice over everything in sight, so that the whole world looked white and pure and beautiful, and full of the lustrous cool fire and perfect clarity of diamonds. I could not hold back a gasp of wonder, but there was more, for the man in white pointed with his sword and there before my eyes I saw a brand new train, one not made of steel but of resplendent silver, waiting on tracks of pure gold that stretched away into infinity, and with an engine that was like a magnificent white horse with a smoke of stars and galaxies steaming from its nostrils. He led me towards it, and soon we were standing beside a coach that was decorated as though for royalty, trimmed with bunting and adorned with all the colors of the rainbow. Climbing inside, I saw that the car was filled with men and women and children who were all dressed in the same sort of brilliant white cape worn by the tall man, just as if they were on their way to some great festival of choirs. The train seemed full of snowy white wings, dancing and shimmering like the clear foaming waters of a mountain stream. Everyone mingled, laughing, singing, celebrating, drinking purple wine from a great crystal bowl at the doorway. And once again I thought: it's Christmas morning!

And then I had yet another surprise—for I looked into the beaming faces of these travelers and recognized them as the same carload of drab emigrants who had been with me on the fearful train ride of the night before. Gone now was any hint of the night's tragedy; all was light and joy, and every face shone like a star. And happiest of all, I thought, were the young parents of the poor little baby I had been so powerless to help. He alone appeared to be absent from our company. And yet there was no trace of grief in the eyes of the young mother, and it was she who met me at the door, took my coat, and replaced it with one of the radiant white garments. And so I joined the others and soon was singing and dancing and rejoicing just as if there never had been any dark train ride in the night, nor any threatening soldiers, nor any such thing as danger or separation or sorrow, nor any tiny baby abandoned under the seat of a railway car.

At the same time, as complete as our joy was, there did seem to remain something hollow in us, something that could not forget the little helpless bundle that had been left behind us in that other world. In fact, I was sure he was uppermost in all of our minds, a more vibrant presence than any other on the train. For who could conceive what tortures he would even now be undergoing, encumbered with all the old useless baggage the rest of us had shed while his train rolled on into some deeper night? What could be more bitter than the torments of unmitigated suffering and abandonment in a wholly innocent heart? We all understood, now, that he was the one the soldiers had been seeking to isolate all along, singling him out for a destiny more terrible than any of the rest of us could ever have borne.

Even as I had these thoughts, however, I caught a glimpse through one of the windows of the tall brilliant man in his refulgent robe climbing astride the great white horse at the head of the train. And pointing his sword at the summit of the sky, he whispered a command in a voice so still, so small, that it seemed eternity stopped to listen.

And then our train began to move.

Apocalyptic Fiction

When He was alone, the Twelve and the others around Him asked Him about the parables. He told them: "The secret of the Kingdom of God has been given to you. But to those on the outside everything is said in parables, so that 'they may be ever seeing but never perceiving, and ever hearing but never understanding. Otherwise they might turn and be forgiven!'"

—MARK 4:10–12

The Bible is in many ways an exasperating, confounding book, often appearing unnecessarily veiled and contradictory. Obviously part of the reason for this is just the terrible complexity of human life. We are not simple, straightforward creatures, and neither are our problems to be treated with pat, simplistic answers. God Himself, of course, is simple. He is the simplest and purest of beings, perfectly uncluttered and therefore disarmingly candid: "In Him there is no darkness at all!" (1 John 1:5). But in man there is darkness, and the human web is an infinitely tangled one. "The heart is deceitful above all things, and desperately wicked!" bemoans Jeremiah. "Who can understand it?" (17:9). Accordingly, in order to address such a hopelessly complex situation, the Bible adopts some complex strategies.

One of these strategies is fiction, or parables. As a bicycle can travel over terrain inaccessible to an automobile, so may a story sometimes wiggle its way into the remotest reaches of the human heart, where the more ponderous vehicle of rational theology cannot always go.

That much is clear enough. Nevertheless, this one rather obvious application of storytelling is not the Bible's final word on the subject. For in the passage from Mark quoted above, it is difficult to escape the conclusion that Jesus' primary purpose in employing stories was not so much that the truth might be communicated in a palatable form to unbelievers, but rather that it might be *deliberately concealed* from them! Far from being an ingenious teaching tool, the parables were meant, it seems, as an intentionally obscurantist tactic. They were to function like smoke screens, thrown up before the faces of the bad guys while the good guys made a clean getaway.

Ultimately, of course, it is never God's desire to pull the wool over anyone's eyes, nor to prevent anyone from hearing the gospel. Indeed Jesus' final miracle before He died was to restore to wholeness the severed ear of one of His enemies (Luke 22:51). But let's face it: we're in a war, a war between good and evil. And in wartime tactics such as discretion, secrecy, and camouflage become of the utmost importance. All messages must be sent in code, and the only decoder for the message of holiness is the Holy Spirit, who is given solely on condition of total surrender to Christ. So "the secret of the Kingdom of God has been given to you," Jesus told His disciples, "but to those on the outside, everything is encoded in parables." For there is a time to reveal oneself and to confront the enemy boldly. But there is also a time for lying low and hiding. There is a time for Christians to be keeping secrets. Parables are one answer to the problem of how God and His people, under conditions of open warfare, may go about proffering a peace treaty to those who are utterly indisposed even to talk about peace, let alone to accept the Lord's unnegotiable terms. And if the Bible appears an obscure and difficult book, it is so that the Devil, together with all those who reject Christ, will be unable to understand it.

"Bound For Glory" is a story that, admittedly, appears to play its cards fairly close to the chest. But "it is the glory of God to conceal a matter" (Prov. 25:2), and perhaps it can be said of this story that its method is that of concealing in order to reveal, of keeping secrets only in order to tell them. If such a story satisfies, it is because it mystifies. It raises questions as a way of answering them.

For instance, one of the central questions raised by the story concerns the identity of the enigmatic soldier, the commanding officer with his great rain cape swishing like a pair of bright wings. What are we to make of the dramatic transformation that comes over this character as the story unfolds? Can an automatic rifle turn into a sword? Can the man on the white horse at the conclusion really be the same person as the ruthless military monster we meet at the outset? And a deeper question: Is there some way in which this man is to be identified with the story's innocent little baby? Or a more probing question still: If we lay our cards on the table and say flatly that the soldier somehow "represents Jesus," why is it that this Jesus comes across more as a cruel Gestapo figure than as a loving Savior? Is the Kingdom of God a reign of terror? And what about the tiny baby? Is he Jesus too? If so, is he the infant Christ or the crucified Christ? Is this a Christmas story or an Easter story?

"Bound For Glory" challenges us, in short, to think about the many names and roles and identities of God, about His different manifestations and His manifold personhood. In the same way the Bible, without ever using the word *Trinity* and without ever stating the Trinitarian doctrine directly, nevertheless conveys to us unmistakably the mystical truth that the Almighty God is three persons in one. Yet how can this be? How can God be both Father and Son, both invisible Spirit and incarnate Word, or both baby and grown man? Or how could God have died?

Well, about all we can say at this point is that the Bible, like life itself, abounds in paradoxes and leaves many burning questions unanswered. At the same time, however, is there not a sense in which the very mysteries of faith turn out to be answers in themselves? As G. K. Chesterton puts it, writing about Job, "Man is most comforted by paradoxes."

Another question raised by "Bound For Glory" concerns its protagonist: Who *is* the protagonist here, and who the antagonist? Classically a protagonist in literature is the principle character of a work, around whom all the action centers, while an antagonist is a figure who in some way opposes this person, frustrating his purposes. In the case of the present story it would seem obvious enough that the principle role is assigned to the unnamed trench-coated traveler through whose eyes all the action is viewed and who continues to the end to occupy center stage. But can it really be said of this man that he functions as the protagonist, the person whom the reader tends not only to "identify with" but to "cheer for"?

Well, yes. At least on a first reading. In retrospect, however, it may happen that the mysterious commanding officer begins to emerge in the reader's mind as an increasingly compelling center of gravity. For is he not the person whose purposes have been resisted all along, opposed by the complacent foreign scholar who initially wanted nothing more out of this trip than to have a seat to himself? Moreover, as this self-important traveler comes under the influence of a little baby, does he himself not begin to surrender some of his own credentials as protagonist and to concede that, far from being the star actor, he is perhaps the one being *acted upon*? "I felt mysteriously," he reflects, "that if anyone had loved [or done anything good at all!] it was not I, but he."

There are, in effect, two powerful literary traditions in conflict here. On the one hand there is the tradition of the classical "hero," the shining-robed, conquering King astride His great white horse, who emerges at the end of the story; and on the other hand there is the modern tradition of the "antihero," the ordinary, snivelling little man whose grandest purpose in life is to get a seat to himself. In a story where these two archetypes meet and clash, which one will emerge as the protagonist, as the true hero?

On the surface of it this question may appear as little more than a nicety of literary criticism. Yet in another way can it perhaps be seen as the central question of the gospel? For in a contemporary world where "real heroes" have vanished, the Christian faith continues to demand a belief not only in heroism but also in a form of heroism that turns all traditional heroics (as well as all modern antiheroics) upside down. So the question posed by the gospel is this: Will modern man, in his sinful antiheroism, allow Jesus Christ to be his true Hero, his King and his Savior? To answer in the affirmative is to name the Lord Jesus as chief Protagonist, not just of the Bible but of life itself, and thus to see in Him the one in whom all the other characters in the pages of the world's novel must seek their identity. More than that, it is to recognize that all other "characters" are essentially *noncharacters*—beings incapable of having any true character at all apart from Him. An acceptance of Christ is a confession that all other human beings are fundamentally *antagonists* of the Lord of Hosts, enemies of life itself, God's bitter opponents who (until such time as they bend the knee before His Son) are actively engaged in sabotaging His purposes at every turn.

Still another literary sort of question that might be asked of "Bound For Glory" concerns the matter of its *genre*. What category of literature is this? Might it, like the other stories in this book, be labeled as *realistic fiction*, or would *science fiction* or *fantasy* be a better term? Or could it be that this is a mixture of genres? If so, is there some point in the story at which the governing mode actually changes from realism to that of fantasy? Or would some other entirely different genre label be appropriate?

These are all questions that are germane to many of Jesus' parables. His stories too have a way of switching gears radically in midstream, so that all of a sudden we can find ourselves catapulted onto a wholly different plane of reality. In Matthew's version of the parable of the wedding banquet, for example, the unremarkable opening has the effect of lulling the listener into accepting a fairly conventional fictional world, in which a king is preparing a feast for the occasion of his son's wedding. What follows, however, as discussed previously, is not a logical sequence of narrative events within this same established order but rather a furious wrenching apart of all normal expectations. True, nothing actually happens that could not, conceivably, happen in the world as we know it, yet at the same time the events are violent and zany enough to satisfy any modern novelist. What sort of literary genre is this?

Or consider another example, the parable of Lazarus and the rich man in Luke 16. As the story opens we are in the "real" world, where a wealthy aristocrat (rich as sin, one might say) lives in the lap of luxury, while day after day right under his nose lies a starving, diseased beggar. Then in the twinkling of an eye the scene changes (or more than the scene, is it the very *genre* that changes at this point?) as in one sentence we are transported into a future, heavenly realm in which the fortunes of these two men have been fantastically reversed. Yet is the change really so fantastic? Has Jesus actually switched to the genre of *fantasy* here, or might it be argued that He is continuing in the mode of *realistic fiction?*

Essentially this is a question not just about literary genre but about the very nature of biblical symbolism. Towards the end of this same parable Jesus says that between Lazarus and the rich man in their eternal abodes, "a great chasm has been fixed, so that those who want to go from here to there cannot, nor can anyone cross over from there to here." In sketching this vivid picture of the "great chasm" it is important to understand that Jesus may not, like Dante or Bunyan, be employing an imaginary, otherworldly geography in which the topographical features are intended to represent spiritual realities. No, more likely the Lord is here speaking not figuratively but literally. He is not "imagining" anything, but rather is referring to something He Himself has seen with His own eyes: the great and uncrossable chasm that is eternally, existentially fixed between Heaven and Hell.

But wait: Why can't this chasm be merely a symbol? Are not words always woefully inadequate to the task of describing spiritual reality? Yes, but the reason for this inadequacy is not to be located in any inherent deficiency of language itself; rather, the poverty of language stems from the inability of human beings to "hear" it. So when Jesus says "chasm," He means precisely that, chasm. He is not just using an analogy (though there is that aspect of it too) but is talking literally about something He Himself spoke into existence from the beginning.

Heaven and Hell, in other words, are not symbolic constructs in Christ's theological system; they are real places. And the same category of supernal reality must apply equally to the Garden of Eden, to cite a further example, and to the mysterious tree in the middle of it from which Adam and Eve ate, and died. This tree was no "mere symbol" (does one die from a symbol?), yet neither was it merely a "literal tree." Rather, it was the *tree of the knowledge of good and evil.* It was as real and as unearthly a thing as the cross on which the Lord of Glory was crucified.

Such is the imponderable mystery behind all biblical symbols. They are, in their own right, staggering realities, and it is their earthly counterparts (whether trees, chasms, jewels, or trumpets) that by comparison pale into insubstantiality. This explains why any thought of labeling Jesus' parables as *fantasy* or *science fiction* must be ruled out. It is also the key to understanding that peculiar genre of religious literature known as *apocalyptic*. For in genres such as fantasy and science fiction it is quite clear that things happen that are beyond the scope of earthly reality. But in apocalyptic writing reality itself is shown up as being inadequate. The normal world is jostled, invaded, revolutionized by something inestimably greater. It is like a big fish swallowing up a smaller: history comes under the judgment of eternity, and before our eyes the kingdoms of this world are transformed into the Kingdom of our God and of His Christ. In the Apocalypse of John, therefore, the author claims that his amazing outpouring of images consists of things not merely *imagined* but *seen*, making this last book of the Bible one in which a densely symbolic, mythopoeic narrative is inextricably bound up with a literal, factual account of the future unfolding of cosmic history. Fact and fiction, in a sense, become one and the same.

What can we say, then, about the story "Bound For Glory"? Is this realism, fantasy, or apocalyptic? On the surface it is a realistic story that becomes, or opens out into, fantasy. But from the Christian perspective surely it must be viewed as being realistic all the way through—or at least as *aspiring* to realism, and therefore to apocalyptic. We need not claim for it the same prophetic stature as the Book of Revelation in order to say that, like so many of the parables of Jesus, this story begins in a rather ordinary setting only to have the Kingdom of Heaven break into it in outlandish ways. Its very effect hinges upon nightmarish twists, improbable crises, sudden eruptions of the absurd and the outrageous.

A tone of horror mixed with the bizarre is characteristic of apocalyptic (and also, it should be noted, of much historical biblical narrative), and ultimately in Scripture all such events point towards the one single most horrifying and bizarre event of all history—the Crucifixion of Christ. This peculiar ambience, moreover, is intended to reflect the chaotic circumstances in the life of any individual (the man in this story, let's say, or you or me) at the critical moment of his or her own personal salvation, that experience of turning from the world and being crucified with Christ. For only in retrospect is the salvation of God a joyous and orderly thing, a grandly efficient military operation like the Exodus. At the time it happens it is steeped in chaos and nightmare.

Ernest Hemingway once wrote that every story, if told long enough, is a "sad story," implying that happy stories are only happy because they withhold, or stop short of, the inevitable final scene, which is always death. But stories of the Kingdom of God go a step further than Hemingway was comfortable with, for God tells His stories even longer, to the point where the tales in the last book of the Bible are of more gargantuanly tragic proportions than anything Hemingway dared to imagine. Only for those who believe is the ultimate outcome of such tales an entirely happy one, an ending in which death and evil are forever vanquished.

This is the function of apocalyptic: it tells the story right to the end, even if the true ending is something that can be known only by faith. Apocalyptic, like a charging locomotive, smashes right through even the end of time as though it were a paper hoop, until finally it can be said that the essence of apocalyptic is the bursting of the bounds of all symbolism. For there can be no symbolism in Heaven—all is pure reality!

"Therefore, write what you have *seen*," the glorified Christ commands John, "what is now and what will take place later" (Rev. 1:19).